THE HOUSE OF THE SEVEN GABLES

Severing Family and Colonial Ties

TWAYNE'S MASTERWORK STUDIES

Robert Lecker, General Editor

THE HOUSE OF THE SEVEN GABLES

Severing Family and Colonial Ties

PETER BUITENHUIS

Twayne Publishers ◇ Boston
A Division of G. K. Hall & Co.

The House of the Seven Gables: Severing Family and Colonial Ties
Peter Buitenhuis

Twayne's Masterwork Studies, No. 66
Copyright 1991 by G. K. Hall & Co.
All rights reserved.
Published by Twayne Publishers
A division of G. K. Hall and Co.
70 Lincoln Street
Boston, Massachusetts 02111

Copyediting supervised by Barbara Sutton.
Book production by Gabrielle B. McDonald.
Typeset in Sabon with Aldus and Arrow display faces
by Compset, Inc. of Beverly, Massachusetts.

10 9 8 7 6 5 4 3 2 1 (hc)
10 9 8 7 6 5 4 3 2 1 (pb)

Printed and bound in the United States of America.

Library of Congress Cataloging-in-Publication Data

Buitenhuis, Peter.
  The House of seven gables : severing family and colonial ties /
Peter Buitenhuis.
      p.   cm.—(Twayne's masterwork studies)
  Includes bibliographical references and index.
  ISBN 0-8057-8075-0.—ISBN 0-8057-8146-3 (pbk.)
  1. Hawthorne, Nathaniel, 1804–1864. House of the seven gables.
  I. Title. II. Series.
  PS1861.B85   1991
  813'.3—dc20   90-25739
                                                      CIP

contents

note on the references and acknowledgments

Parenthetical page references to *The House of the Seven Gables* are from the Norton Critical Edition (NCE): *The House of the Seven Gables: An Authoritative Text, Backgrounds and Sources, Essays in Criticism*, edited by Seymour L. Gross (New York: W. W. Norton, 1967). This edition uses the text of the novel prepared for volume 2 of *The Centenary Edition of the Works of Nathaniel Hawthorne*, edited by William Charvat (Columbus: Ohio State University Press, 1965), and is therefore the most authoritative available. Quotations from Hawthorne's letters are from volume 16 of this edition, *The Letters*, edited by Thomas Woodson, L. Neal Smith, and Norman Holmes Pearson (Columbus: Ohio State University Press, 1985). Excerpts from both volumes are reprinted by permission of Ohio State University Press.

For other works by Hawthorne, I have used *The Works of Nathaniel Hawthorne*, 13 vols. (Boston: Houghton Mifflin, 1883). References to this edition are cited in the text as *Works* and are followed by volume and page numbers.

I am grateful to Robert Lecker who provided me with the opportunity to undertake this work, which turned out to be both challenging and rewarding; it revealed more richness in this novel than I had dreamed of. In preparation for this study I owe much to the conscientious work of Irwin Shubert, my research assistant on a Simon Fraser work-study grant. He ferreted out and read through the voluminous secondary sources on Hawthorne and also put together the chronology. My wife, Ann Cowan, read and commented on the manuscript and, as she has done so often before, brought her unfailing eagle eye to my lacunae, lapses of logic, and errors of expression. She is as good an editor as she is a partner.

Nathaniel Hawthorne
Photograph by Matthew Brady

chronology: nathaniel hawthorne's life and works

1804	Nathaniel Hawthorne born on the Fourth of July in Union Street house, Salem, Massachusetts, the only son of Nathaniel Hathorne (sea captain, b. 1775) and Elizabeth Clarke Manning (b. 1780). Sisters Elizabeth (Ebe), born 1802, died 1883; and Maria Louisa, born 1808, died 1852.
1808	Father dies en route to Surinam, Dutch East Indies.
1809	The Hathorne family moves to the Manning home on Herbert Street, Salem.
1811	Nathaniel attends Joseph Worcester's school.
1813	Injures his foot. Consequently his schooling is interrupted and he pursues a great deal of solitary reading, along with private tutoring. He does not completely recover from this injury until he is twelve years old. His grandfather Manning dies on a journey to the family lands in Raymond, Maine. Richard Manning, Hawthorne's uncle, moves to Raymond to oversee the sale of the family estate; he never returns to Salem.
1816	Mrs. Hawthorne and the children move to Raymond in the summer.
1818	Hawthorne returns to Salem to study, but his mother and sisters remain in Raymond.
1819	On 5 July, the day after his fifteenth birthday, Hawthorne begins to study at Mr. Archer's School on Marlboro Street.
1820	Leaves Archer's school in March to prepare for college entrance, under the tutelage of Benjamin L. Oliver, a Salem lawyer.
1821–1825	Attends Bowdoin College, Brunswick, Maine, where he studies Greek, Latin, mathematics (astronomy, surveying, navigation), and philosophy (Christian apologetics).
1822	Mother returns to Salem, giving up residence in Raymond.

1824	Marriage of uncle, Robert Manning, to Elizabeth Dodge Burnham.
1825–1837	After leaving college, Hawthorne remains secluded in the attic of his mother's house. Although he maintains contact with the outside world, his main objective is to master the art of writing.
1828	Publishes anonymously, and at his own expense, *Fanshawe: A Tale*. Robert Manning builds a house for Mrs. Hawthorne, next to his own at 16 Dearborn Street, where family lives for the next four years.
1830–1837	Hawthorne publishes several tales and sketches in various magazines, either anonymously or under pseudonyms.
1836	Becomes editor of the *American Magazine of Useful and Entertaining Knowledge*.
1837	Publishes *Twice-Told Tales* and *Peter Parley's Universal History*, the latter part of a children's series all supposedly written by Samuel Goodrich, entitled "Peter Parley."
1838	Becomes engaged to Sophia Peabody.
1839–1840	Measurer of coal and salt at the Boston Customhouse.
1841	Publishes *Grandfather's Chair*. Lives at Brook Farm from April to November.
1842	Marries Sophia Peabody in Boston, 9 July. Robert Manning dies, 10 October. Second edition, enlarged, of *Twice-Told Tales*.
1842–1845	Resides at the Old Manse, Concord, Massachusetts.
1844	Daughter Una born.
1845	Editor of Horatio Bridge's *Journal of an African Cruiser*.
1846	Son Julian born. *Mosses from an Old Manse*.
1846–1849	Surveyor to the Port of Salem.
1849	Mother dies.
1850	*The Scarlet Letter*.
1850–1851	Lives in Lenox, Massachusetts, where he gets to know Herman Melville.
1851	Daughter Rose born. *The House of the Seven Gables*, *The Snow Image*, and *True Stories from History and Biography*.
1851–1852	Lives in West Newton, Massachusetts.
1852	Franklin Pierce elected president of the United States. *The Life of Franklin Pierce*, *The Blithedale Romance* and *A Wonder Book for Girls and Boys*.

Chronology: Nathaniel Hawthorne's Life and Works

1852–1853   Lives at the Wayside, Concord, Massachusetts.

1853   Sister Maria Louisa dies following an explosion of a Hudson River steamer. *Tanglewood Tales for Girls and Boys*.

1853–1857   Appointed by Franklin Pierce as consul in Liverpool, England.

1857–1859   Lives in Rome and Florence.

1859   Returns to England and lives in Redcar, Yorkshire.

1860   *The Marble Faun*. Returns to the United States and to the Wayside in Concord.

1861   American Civil War begins.

1863   *Our Old Home*, dedicated to Franklin Pierce.

1864   Dies in the company of Franklin Pierce at Concord, New Hampshire. Buried in Concord, Massachusetts, 23 May, leaving manuscripts of four uncompleted romances.

Literary and Historical Context

1

Life and Letters

Nathaniel Hawthorne was a child of New England Puritans, and all his work reflects his inheritance. A scion of one of the oldest families in the country, he grew up and remained for many years in one of the earliest Puritan settlements on the New England coast, the port town of Salem, Massachusetts. Before and during his lifetime, however, the port lost more and more of its trade to Boston. Salem increasingly took on the aspect of a maritime backwater. Hawthorne's family fell on hard times after his father, a sea captain, died of fever on his way to the East Indies when Nathaniel was only four years old. Support for the family, however, came from Hawthorne's mother's relations, the Mannings.

Nathaniel grew up fatherless and dependent on relations who were hardworking, prosperous, and materialistic. Hawthorne, on the contrary, was a dreamy, imaginative, and often indolent boy, who, as a youth, decided he wanted to become a writer. Faced with both his Puritan inheritance and the business enterprise of his mother's family, however, he was continually plagued by the feeling that such a career would be frivolous, even worthless.

When he was seventeen, he was dispatched by the family to Bow-doin College in Maine, where it was expected that he would develop some skills that would fit him for a career. His studies, however, only confirmed him in his desire to write. On leaving college, instead of looking for a job, Hawthorne holed up in his mother's house and worked for twelve years at developing his craft. He avidly read classical mythology and New England history and soaked up the English classics. He was particularly influenced by the allegorical styles of Spenser's *Faerie Queen* and Bunyan's *The Pilgrim's Progress*. The Puritan power of Milton's *Paradise Lost* made a profound impression on him as did Shakespeare's comedies and tragedies. He also read the English romantic poets and novelists and the popular writers of his day. In 1828 he privately published a Gothic novel, *Fanshawe*. He then wrote a series of short tales that were published anonymously or under various names in various periodicals. A friend persuaded him to collect these works into a volume. Published in 1837, when Hawthorne was thirty-three, *Twice-Told Tales* was his first significant public appearance.

Hawthorne had realized by then that he could not make a living as a writer of tales and felt that he had to try other occupations in order to cease being what he called "the obscurest man-of-letters in America." He turned to various kinds of literary hackwork and became an editor of the popular *Magazine of Useful and Entertaining Knowledge*. The need to increase his income was made more pressing when he fell in love and became engaged to Sophia Peabody. He was a strong supporter of the Democratic party, and, fortunately, some political friendships he had made while at college led to an appointment to the Boston Customhouse as a measurer of coal and salt. He gave up this dreary job in 1840. There followed an unsatisfactory stint of eight months with a group of Utopian visionaries at Brook Farm. This experience was the source for the later ironical and satirical novel, *The Blithedale Romance*.

In 1842, he made two brave decisions: after a courtship of four years, at the age of thirty-eight, he married Sophia; he also determined to try once more to become a professional writer and moved into the Old Manse at Concord—then the center of American literary activity. There he met members of the Concord school of transcendentalists, including Bronson Alcott, Ralph Waldo Emerson, and Henry David Thoreau. Emerson and Hawthorne never saw eye to eye; their views of life could not have been more different. Emerson was optimistic, future oriented, philosophical, and individualistic. Hawthorne was mostly pessimistic, obsessed with the past, instinctual, imaginative, and deeply aware of the power of social mores and convention. Hawthorne felt more attuned to Thoreau, admiring his freedom, his learning and good sense, even though he found Thoreau intolerant, limited, and unmalleable. But, like both Emerson and Thoreau, Hawthorne was essentially solitary and could not subscribe to any of the current forms of organized religion. Like them, he was also steeped in the Bible and shared a Puritan tradition that led to a belief in the preeminence of spirit over matter. This religious inheritance led Hawthorne toward the use of symbolism in his work—a practice that he shared with the transcendentalists and other writers of the American renaissance.

The transcendentalist school did not go in much for fiction. Indeed, when Hawthorne looked for American predecessors in his chosen artistic form, he could find little to help him. James Fenimore Cooper's romantic novels demonstrate what can be done with native material, but his hastily written and improvised narratives held little appeal for the craftsman in Hawthorne. Washington Irving is a better example of how American local legends can be shaped by literary artistry, but his work mostly takes the form of the sketch, and Hawthorne was more interested in longer fictional forms. Charles Brockden Brown, who died in 1811, gives guidance on how the English Gothic romance tradition can be adapted to American sensibilities, although his work has a melodramatic cast too strong for Hawthorne's taste. *Fanshawe*, Hawthorne's first novel, owes less to American than to British sources: the romances of Sir Walter Scott and William Godwin.

Hawthorne faced a greater problem than finding an appropriate tradition and form: he needed to find a market for his work. Outlets for professional writers then were few, and the lack of effective copyright laws made protecting literary property practically impossible. Because his family was growing (two children were born, in 1844 and

1846), he was forced to seek other employment and, again through political influence, he was appointed in 1846 as surveyor for the port of Salem. Since the port by this time was the destination for very few ships, this appeared to be a safe sinecure that admirably fitted his naturally indolent temperament. His complacency was, however, rudely shattered when, after three years, a new political administration came to power. Along with many other easygoing denizens of the Customhouse, he was fired.

This shock proved highly beneficial to Hawthorne's career; he buckled down at once to his creative work and, writing as much as nine hours a day, produced *The Scarlet Letter* in six months. Soon after its publication Hawthorne met Herman Melville, a mutual admirer who had already written an enthusiastic article on Hawthorne's short stories; Hawthorne had also read Melville's early work, and written a short favorable review of *Typee*. The two men immediately hit it off and there is little doubt that their association gave both a shot of creative energy. During the next two years Hawthorne published *The House of the Seven Gables* (1851) and *The Blithedale Romance* (1852) and Melville published *Moby-Dick* (1851) and *Pierre* (1852). As an acknowledgment of his debt, Melville dedicated *Moby-Dick* to Hawthorne. In his earlier review of the short stories he had, without apology, compared Hawthorne to Shakespeare, and then gone on to make what still remains the most profound statement about Hawthorne. In comparing the author's work to that of Emerson, Melville observed: "this great power of blackness [in Hawthorne] derives its force from its appeals to that Calvinistic sense of Innate Depravity and Original Sin, from whose visitations, in some shape or other, no deeply thinking mind is always and wholly free. . . . Perhaps no writer has ever wielded this terrific thought with greater terror than this same harmless Hawthorne."[1]

This notation offers a key to the interpretation of *The House of the Seven Gables*, which is, like *The Scarlet Letter*, a study in the effects of sin on the individual mind and on posterity. Sophia Hawthorne had been dismayed by the darkness and terror of *The Scarlet Letter*. Urged on by his wife, Hawthorne made a conscious decision to write a happier book, one that would represent the more relaxed tenor of his own times. *The House of the Seven Gables* is, consequently, much lighter in tone and has a much happier outcome than its predecessor. Nonetheless, the later novel unmistakably dramatizes similar preoccupations about the human condition and reflects its author's continuing obsession with sin and moral depravity.

Despite his disclaimer in the preface that the novel should "be read strictly as a Romance," Hawthorne took great pains over the realistic detail in *The House of the Seven Gables*. He minutely represents the materiality of the contemporary world and something of the decayed splendor of a once flourishing port town. As in *The Scarlet Letter,* however, the spiritual power finally prevails over the material.

I believe that in *The House of the Seven Gables* Hawthorne strikes out on a new path with the romance form. Dissatisfied with the historical fantasies of both Sir Walter Scott and James Fenimore Cooper, and also with what he called in his preface, "the minute fidelity" required by the novel, he still wanted the freedom to deal with how history lives on into the present. He therefore claimed the latitude of the romancer while using the resources of the realist to construct a fiction that is at once imaginative, even fanciful, and also represents a real, recognizable world. The resources of allegory and symbolism that he derived from his Puritan heritage blended with his strong powers of mimesis to produce his richest, most various and delightful work.

2

The Importance of the Work

During Hawthorne's lifetime *The House of the Seven Gables* was generally considered the best of his novels. Time has revised this estimate: *The Scarlet Letter* is now universally held to be his greatest work. *The House of the Seven Gables,* however, is still generally ranked second among his works. Hawthorne's contemporaries praised most of all its richness and readability. Indeed, the review by Evert Duyckinck is as relevant today as it was in 1851:

> It is not a shilling novel that you are purchasing when you buy The House of the Seven Gables, but a book—a book with lights and shades, parts and diversities, upon which you may feed and pasture, not exhausting the whole field at an effort, but returning now and then to uncropped fairy rings and bits of herbage. You may read the book into the small hours beyond midnight, when no sound breaks the silence but the parting of an expiring ember, or the groan of restless mahogany, and you find that the candle burns a longer flame, and that the ghostly visions of the author's page take shape about you. Conscience sits supreme in her seat, the fountains of pity and terror are opened; you look into the depths of the soul, provoked at so painful a sight—but you are strengthened as you gaze; for of that pain comes peace at last, and these shadows you must master by virtuous magic.[1]

The Importance of the Work

Embers may no longer expire, nor mahogany groan, nor candles burn in our living rooms, but Hawthorne's magic still holds sway under the reading lamp as the ghostly visions of his characters parade before us and the image of the decaying house prints itself on our memory. Duyckinck was also right to evoke the traditional Aristotelian tragic qualities of pity and terror, for Hawthorne, like Sophocles, Euripides, and Aeschylus, deals with men and women caught in the toils of fate.

Similarly, as Eugene O'Neill would later do in his great trilogy *Mourning Becomes Electra,* Hawthorne blends the classical tragic theme of the family curse with New England Puritan history to create a powerful drama about how pride and ambition are brought to a downfall. But in his characterization Hawthorne treated this ancient theme with his own peculiar blend of irony and humor. Judge Pyncheon, one of Hawthorne's great creations of character, is no tragic hero, but a selfish, narrow, obsessed man who has dressed his ambition in the guise of benevolence. Scarcely less impressive are the portraits of the repressed, shy, virginal, rusty old spinster, Hepzibah; the neurotic, fearful, and poetic Clifford; and Holgrave, the unheroic hero.

Hawthorne works brilliantly with chiaroscuro in *The House of the Seven Gables.* The dark old house and the darkened characters are contrasted with light—the play of sunshine lighting up the rooms and the garden, and the childlike brightness of Phoebe spreading a flow of happiness wherever she runs. This chiaroscuro is linked with the symbolism in an intricate pattern of effects. On a fairly literal level, the chiaroscuro is given symbolic expression by Holgrave's occupation as a daguerreotypist. Daguerreotype is a photographic process by which a silver-coated plate is exposed for a time to sunlight. The image is then covered, fixed with chemicals, and put in darkness until it develops. Symbolism works throughout the novel on many levels: from the absurdly comic—the dwarfish chickens—to the portentously tragic—the fatal draft of blood.

The whole novel can be described as a working out in fictional form of Emerson's famous definition in *Nature,* that "particular natural facts are signs of particular spiritual facts." From this root belief,

Hawthorne developed his symbolic fiction by a series of what Melville called in *Moby-Dick*, "linked analogies." Hawthorne creates a picture of a moral universe in which past cannot be separated from present, nor causes from their consequences, nor objects from their significance, nor characters from their intrinsic moral meaning. Moreover, in this novel Hawthorne creates a new version of Gothic romance: American Gothic, for his earlier contemporary, Edgar Allan Poe, had set his Gothic romances in Europe.

One major achievement of *The House of the Seven Gables* is that it provides an understanding of the Puritan conscience as it operated in mid–nineteenth-century Massachusetts and incidentally gives a valid historical glimpse of New England society at that time—a society in decay, yet with prospects of change and renewal. Although the end of the novel is ambiguous, the dead hand of the past, for which Hawthorne had both a healthy respect and a deep distrust, is in part lifted; as Duyckinck says, aptly, "of that pain comes peace at last."

With his usual felicity of phrase, Henry James best sums up the achievement of *The House of the Seven Gables*: "It is a large and generous production, pervaded with that vague hum, that indefinable echo, of the whole multitudinous life of man, which is the real sign of a great work of fiction."[2]

3

Critical Reception

What is the point of looking at the critical history of a work of literature—that is to say, at the way it has been received by generations of readers? Each age has to reevaluate the classics and read them in the light of its own cultural and critical assumptions, which gradually change over time. The way we read *The House of the Seven Gables* will not be the same as the way Hawthorne's contemporaries read it, or the way readers in 1920 or 1950 read it. Yet looking at earlier interpretations helps us gain a sense of the cumulative richness of the text over time.

There is no "right" way to interpret a text, although some interpretations will be better informed than others. Interpretation justifies itself by bringing something external to the work—another way of looking at the artist's creation. If that interpretation is very subjective—that is, if it relates more to the reader's values and ideas than to the writer's—chances are the interpretation will be flawed. On the other hand, if that subjectivity is in itself creatively brilliant, such as D. H. Lawrence's eccentric work in *Studies in Classic American Literature*, then that interpretation will add something of value.

There is never an end to interpretation. Each time a book is read, it is a different book, for it is re-created in the mind of the reader. Even when it is reread, it is re-created. The most important response, then, is *your* response as a reader, and that response should be your first guide. The reading of other responses will help clarify and extend your sense of a text. Sometimes a critical reading will act as a starting block for you to take off on your own critical run; sometimes it will act as a wall against which you want to bounce off your own contrary ideas.

Over the years, new disciplines have given rise to new interpretations. The social science of anthropology, for example, gave a spur to the use of myth in interpretation, for the research of anthropologists revealed how important to any culture are its myths of creation, sexuality, death, and salvation. Similarly, Freudian and Jungian psychology gave rise to a whole new school of literary readings, as critics used texts as a means of not only examining the psychology of their authors but also showing how universal patterns of family, gender, and sexual conflicts permeate texts. More recently, the rise of women's studies has led to reinterpretations of classic texts in the light of how women have been interpreted, or misinterpreted, or entirely ignored by male authors.

Given the continual nature of the critical exercise, it is tempting to ask, is there any progress in criticism, or is it simply a great turning wheel without forward direction? In the twentieth century there has been a move away from descriptive criticism to more and more analytical work, and more and more refinement of analytical instruments. We have had great system builders, such as I. A. Richards with his insistence on looking closely at the text and only at the text, which gave rise to the New Criticism. Northrop Frye has established in *Anatomy of Criticism* a subtle and complex system for placing all literary works into certain genres and archetypal forms and establishing intricate networks between them.

Recently a movement called structuralism, related to efforts in the sciences and social sciences to replace atomistic and individualistic thought by more structural and more universal patterns, has attempted to make criticism more scientific and systematic. In the field of literature, structuralism began with the study of the laws of language. Moving from language to literature, structuralism has in particular sought to relate literary works to the whole field of literature and culture of which they are a part. A danger of this scientific approach to literature is that it may create systematic completeness where it does not—cannot—exist. For in the end, the making and the reading of literature are personal, subjective acts that can never be reduced to a system. There is no substitute for the "liking" or "disliking" of a literary work. We must try to achieve in reading any good work of literature a sufficient knowledge of the text so as to be able to justify our preference.

CRITICISM IN HAWTHORNE'S LIFETIME

Turning to *The House of the Seven Gables,* there can be no doubt that Nathaniel Hawthorne liked it the best of all his works. His preference was shared by many of his contemporaries. The critical history of the novel includes the work of some of the best critics and novelists of the whole period and shows that the novel has continued to be held in high esteem. The majority of writers since Hawthorne's time, however, have ranked it behind *The Scarlet Letter.*

Hawthorne's contemporaries on the whole agreed with Evert Duyckinck, some of whose words of praise I quoted earlier. Rufus Griswold, the biographer who is now largely remembered for his malicious and inaccurate attack on Edgar Allan Poe, also thought that *The House of the Seven Gables* was no less original, powerful, and striking than *The Scarlet Letter.* He praises the characterization and concludes that it is "the purest piece of imagination in our prose literature."[1] Unfortunately Poe did not live to see the publication of *Seven Gables,* but he had generously praised Hawthorne's *Twice-Told Tales,* although he had attacked Hawthorne's use of allegory.

The most sympathetic review that *The House of the Seven Gables* received, and the one most appreciated by Hawthorne, was part of a larger article on his work by the poet and critic Henry T. Tuckerman in the *Southern Literary Messenger.* Tuckerman pays a glowing tribute to Hawthorne's style, noting that the author never resorts to tricks of rhetoric or verbal ingenuity. For Hawthorne, he writes, "language is . . . a crystal medium through which to let us see the play of his humor, the glow of his sympathy, and the truth of his observation."[2] In Tuckerman Hawthorne had found his perfect reader, for in a letter written shortly after the publication of *The House of the Seven Gables,* Hawthorne observed: "The greatest possible merit of style is, of course, to make the mere words absolutely disappear into the thought" (*Letters,* 16:421).

Of course, not all the reviewers were united in their praise of *The House of the Seven Gables.* While conceding that it was, taken as a whole, Hawthorne's greatest work, the reviewer in *Graham's Magazine* thought that it lacked unity; there was "a slight fitfulness" toward the conclusion, and "the supernaturally grotesque element" detracted from its integrity.[3] Similarly the reviewer in the famous British journal the *Athenaeum,* while maintaining that Hawthorne ranked "amongst the most original and complete novelists that have appeared in modern times," deplored as "frivolous and vexatious" the "affluence of fancy" that made Hawthorne dwell at length upon the corpse of Judge Pyncheon sitting daylong in the old house.[4]

FROM HAWTHORNE'S DEATH TO 1914

Soon after Hawthorne's death in 1864, and prompted in part by the posthumous publication of his notebooks, critics began to evaluate his place in the pantheon of American writers. As has often been the case with American writers, the most searching early assessments were made by British critics. In an article in *St. Paul's Magazine,* William Brighty Rand ranked Hawthorne first among American writers, although he conceded that some would say that Whitman was more deserving of the place of honor. In a survey of Hawthorne's fiction Rand carefully pointed to the author's use of language and his sense of American history and traditions as particularly "American." Rand criticized Hawthorne, however, for his "inconclusiveness" and "indeterminateness," for what he called his lack of "speculative force." "In Hawthorne's mind," he wrote, "everything seemed capable of meaning something else."[5] Paradoxically, in modern criticism, it is just this sense of ambiguity that has often been cited as the source of Hawthorne's greatest power.

In an essay written in 1872 for the *Cornhill Magazine,* the noted British critic Leslie Stephen also took up the question of Hawthorne's peculiarly American qualities. He discussed the issue at length and decided that this Americanness was most obvious in what he called the "humorous struggle between his sense of the rawness and ugliness of his native land and the dogged patriotism befitting a descendant of the genuine New England Puritans."[6] The American cast of Hawthorne's mind was also evident, Stephen believed, in his interest in psychic phenomena, as opposed to the beefy realism of the British novelists. These preoccupations were part of his peculiar interest. "No modern writer" Stephen claimed, "has the same skill in so using the marvellous as to interest without unduly exciting our incredulity" (Stephen, 501). In combining Yankee practicality with nervous sensitivity, Hawthorne was, thought Stephen, "a characteristic embodiment of true national tendencies" (Stephen, 503).

The British novelist Anthony Trollope, in a general survey of Hawthorne's work published in the *North American Review,* generously extolled Hawthorne's genius but considered *The House of the Seven Gables* quite inferior to *The Scarlet Letter.* Although he thought some of the characters were well drawn, he found Phoebe and Holgrave unconvincing, and the ending of the novel quite out of character, as if it had been added by some "beef-and-ale, realistic novelist."[7] This was a deliberately aimed ironic comment, because Hawthorne had, years before, written that Trollope's own novels had been written "on strength of beef and through the inspiration of ale."[8]

Henry James was a young writer trying to make his name on the English literary scene when he wrote his little book, *Hawthorne,* in 1879. Consequently he patronized his "provincial" countryman from a lofty, cosmopolitan point of view. He called *The House of the Seven Gables* "a magnificent fragment," but went on to lavish considerable praise on its "ethereal beauties" and its charm, which he characterized as "like that of the sweetness of a piece of music, or the softness of fine September weather"; he lavished attention on its characterization, and called it "a large and generous production."[9]

CRITICISM BETWEEN THE WARS

Most nineteenth-century critics emphasized the characterization and the historic, antiquarian, and stylistic aspects of *The House of the Seven Gables*. To a new generation of writers after the First World War Hawthorne was considered a far more substantial figure in American letters than his contemporaries, not for the aforementioned qualities but largely because of his tragic sensibilities and his artistry. T. S. Eliot thought that Hawthorne had a stronger sense of the past than did Henry James. He wrote in an essay in the *Athenaeum* in 1919 that Hawthorne "had . . . what no one else in Boston had—the firmness, the true coldness, the hard coldness of the genuine artist." In discussing *The House of the Seven Gables*, Eliot observed that the novel "has solidity, has permanence, the permanence of art."[10] These were, of course, precisely the qualities that Eliot was trying to achieve in his own art.

In his revolutionary *Studies in Classic American Literature* (1923), D. H. Lawrence unmasked the seemingly innocent Hawthorne and found behind the mask a writer who delved deeply into the black heart of man. "You *must* look through the surface of American art," he wrote, "and see the inner diabolism of the symbolic meaning. Otherwise it is all mere childishness."[11] Lawrence, with the hyperbole typical of his critical judgments, thought that beside *The Scarlet Letter* Hawthorne's other books, including *Seven Gables,* were nothing. He made fun of the new generation who had come to sweep out the ghosts from the old house with a vacuum cleaner, and scorned his "vendetta-born young couple"—Phoebe and Holgrave—who effect "a perfect understanding under the black cloth of a camera and prosperity. *Vivat Industria*" (Lawrence, 104).

Lawrence's remarks recall the long-forgotten comments of Herman Melville in his 1850 review of *Mosses from an Old Manse,* in which he talked of the "blackness of darkness" beyond the apparent sunlight. "In one word," Melville wrote, "the world is mistaken in this Nathaniel Hawthorne. He himself must often have smiled at its absurd misconception of him. He is immeasurably deeper than the plummet of the mere critic."[12]

CRITICISM FROM WORLD WAR II TO 1960

The upsurge of American studies after the end of World War II brought Hawthorne's fiction to the forefront of literary studies, a position that it has subsequently retained. F. O. Matthiessen's groundbreaking *American Renaissance* (1941), written during the dark days of World War II, pointed the way for other critics. Matthiessen was concerned to find a "literature for our democracy," so he put the works of the great nineteenth-century American writers in a rich cultural context. Characteristically, Matthiessen placed an emphasis in his interpretation of *Seven Gables* on the waning of the aristocracy and the solidly based growth of common life and democratic institutions.

Matthiessen analyzes brilliantly how Hawthorne evolved his main theme not so much from the original curse on the house by Matthew Maule as from the curse that the Pyncheons have brought upon themselves through their obsessive desire to build up real estate and other forms of wealth, or what Hawthorne calls "the energy of disease" (23) that has held the Pyncheons in an inflexible grasp. It is not so much their gold and hereditary position that have damned them as their inescapable traits of character. Against the weight of the past, Matthiessen notes, Hawthorne presents his spirit of the democratic present, the jack-of-all trades, Holgrave, "a detailed portrait of one of Emerson's promising Young Americans."[13] Matthiessen considers the end of the novel a failure, because, he believes, Hawthorne's naïve confidence in the continuance of democratic opportunity leads the author to overlook "that he was sowing all over again the same seeds of evil" (Matthiessen, 332). Matthiessen was writing as a democratic socialist and therefore denying Hawthorne's more conservative conviction that property and capital in themselves are not evil. Hawthorne believed that responsible administration of capital by individuals led to the public good. He portrayed in Holgrave a man of integrity who would put wealth to work in ways very different from those employed by the grasping Pyncheons.

It has become more and more noticeable in the Hawthorne criticism since World War II that, like Matthiessen, critics have imposed their particular beliefs on Hawthorne's fiction—fiction that is singularly free of doctrine and certainty. One of the most influential critical strains was begun by Randall Stewart in his finely written biography of Hawthorne, published in 1948.[14] Stewart based his interpretation of Hawthorne on his belief that as a child of the Puritans, Hawthorne followed in essence their orthodoxy and produced work that was both Christian and tragic. Many critics followed Stewart in this Christian orthodox interpretation, including Richard Harter Fogle in *Hawthorne's Fiction: The Light and the Dark* (1952), and Hyatt H. Waggoner in *Hawthorne, a Critical Study* (1955). Waggoner writes of *The House of the Seven Gables* that it can be read in many ways, but that it should be interpreted most of all in the light of the preface, which means, according to Waggoner, that the romance provides "texts for sermons on the sins of pride and avarice and on the fact of mutability, illustrating meanwhile the ways of providence" (Waggoner, 162). He notes at the end of his discussion of the novel that the modern reader, skeptical about Hawthorne's belief in the redemptive power of married love and in immortality, is unable to take the ending of the novel seriously. But this, he says, is a failure of understanding on the part of the reader. "As a mythopoetic fiction," Waggoner concludes, "[*Seven Gables*] is one of the greatest works in American literature."[15]

Shortly after the neoorthodox critics began their work on Hawthorne, the myth critics also began their reevaluation. Taking their cue from D. H. Lawrence, they were primarily interested in establishing a native American mythology. In his influential study *The American*

Adam: Innocence, Tragedy, and Tradition in the Nineteenth Century (1955), R. W. B. Lewis[16] uses Holgrave's diatribe against the past as a text for the American belief in progress, in "the sloughing off of the old skin," to use Lawrence's phrase. Lewis also cites Clifford's "Adamic ambition"—that is, his desire to begin anew—in seeking to leave the past behind when he makes his railroad journey.[16] Lewis notes, however, that the escapes of both Holgrave and Clifford are circular: they both end in return. The Adamic impulses, then, are treated ironically.

In another influential study, *Love and Death in the American Novel* (1960), Leslie Fiedler attempts to reveal in a Lawrentian way "the dangerous and disturbing books" in the canon of American literature. He is also concerned with the way American authors often undercut the effect of their own anarchic strains by resorting to the sentimental tradition of the European novel. So for Fiedler the ending of *The House of the Seven Gables* is Hawthorne's attempt to relieve the gloom of his greatest novel, *The Scarlet Letter,* by reverting to the sentimental tradition. In seeking to make marriage another, better Eden, with woman as the innocent savior capable of restoring man to paradise, the ending rejects, Fiedler says, the "blackness ten times black" that Melville found in Hawthorne in favor of a positive view of life that often tempts American authors, and that condemns them to subsequent failure.[17]

THE HOUSE OF SEVEN GABLES
AND THE PSYCHOLOGISTS

Given Hawthorne's concern for psychology, it was inevitable that Freudian critics should turn their attention to his work. The most notable of these has been Frederick Crews, who begins *The Sins of the Fathers* (1966) by attacking "the timid little revolution" in Hawthorne criticism by those who read him in terms of religious didacticism and symbolism. He denies the "evidence" read into the novels by critics who would turn Hawthorne into "an odd combination of plodding democrat and religious tutor."[18] Like Lewis and Fiedler, Crews goes back to Melville to get at the dark and demonic side of Hawthorne's genius.

The origins of this darkness, according to Crews, lie in the mixture of guilt and pride that Hawthorne felt in the sins and achievements of his ancestors, which included incest on the Manning side as well as witch-hunting on the Hawthorne side. For Crews, *The House of the Seven Gables* is about "the risks of artistic imagination, which are simply the risks of seizure by unconscious wishes" (Crews, 173). The Maule-Pyncheon antagonism, Crews goes on to argue, "is chiefly a metaphor of imperfect repression" (Crews, 178); the antagonism felt toward the father figure in the Oedipal situation is repressed. Even after the death of Judge Pyncheon, Crews maintains, they are pathetic in their attempts to enjoy their newfound freedom. Holgrave, too, is caught up in this fear of and guilt about the father figure and he turns to Phoebe after encountering Jaffrey's corpse, seeking a way out of "the shapeless gloom" that the sight of the body has cast over him. Phoebe, "the embodied negation of all unpleasant fantasies about women" (Crews, 190), can lead both Clifford and Holgrave away from this gloom. But to "become free of anxiety," says Crews, "is to lose all reason for creativity" (Crews, 192). This surrender to the false idealism of the sentimental tradition, Crews claims, agreeing with Fiedler, marks the beginning of the failure of Hawthorne's later career.

Crews's reading of Hawthorne has been attacked for its reductionism, as has much psychoanalytic criticism. This charge means that the work of literature is reduced drastically in its range of meaning and its possibilities by a particular bias or ideology. I would agree that Crews fails to do justice to either the genre that Hawthorne was working in or the variety of Hawthorne's sources. On the other hand, Crews is not a doctrinaire Freudian and his subtle reading of texts brings new insights and reveals new depths in *The House of the Seven Gables*. He does much to correct the image of Hawthorne as an orthodox and moralistic Christian.

Hugo McPherson was among those who felt that Crews took insufficient notice of Hawthorne's literary sources or of the nature of his personality. McPherson has attempted to address these questions by studying both Hawthorne's personal psychology and his knowledge of classical myth in his *Hawthorne as Mythmaker* (1969).[19] McPherson takes myth criticism into the realm of what he called Hawthorne's personal mythology, or "life as allegory." He notes that as early as his college days, Hawthorne called himself Oberon, the fairy from *A Midsummer Night's Dream*. Menaced by his aged "fathers"—his Puritan ancestors—he went on a twelve-year quest of spectres in his fiction, returning to claim his place and marry his princess (Sophia).

As Hawthorne reveals in the Customhouse preface to *The Scarlet Letter*, he, as an artist, felt alienated not only from the past but also from his own society. McPherson maintains that Hawthorne's analysis of New England history in his fiction is an attempt to discover the historical process that produced the America of his own day. He dreamed the American dream as ardently as any patriot, McPherson claims, particularly the dream envisioned by the early Puritans and by Jefferson in the Declaration of Independence. But Hawthorne wondered if in the materialism of the present this dream could ever be realized. In the conclusion to *The House of the Seven Gables*, he was able to hope that a better age was at hand, and that America had exorcised the ghosts of the past.

McPherson points out that those who have read Hawthorne as a Christian moralist recognize the Puritan opposition between reason and passion, head and heart, but fail to take account of Hawthorne's alliance with the romantics, who regarded imagination as the supreme instrument of vision, whereas the Puritans equated imagination not with Oberon's magic but with witchcraft and demonism. In Hawthorne's personal mythology, however, the Heart is flanked by two suitors, "the empirical, daylight faculty of Reason and the nocturnal, magical power of imagination" (McPherson, 11). The problem of the artist in devoting himself to the power of the imagination, however, is that in so doing he may cut himself off from human fellowship, and in his detachment commit the unpardonable sin of prying into the human heart—thus becoming a kind of wizard. For Hawthorne the means of rejoining the human community was through his marriage to Sophia.

Thus *The House of the Seven Gables* is a natural centerpiece for McPherson's thesis because it reveals, he says, that Hawthorne's imagination was deeply informed by the Greek myths that Hawthorne read widely during his twelve-year seclusion after college. The Judge is the tyrannical father figure, associated with the sun and with iron, and explicitly compared to Midas, while the house itself is a double image, on the one hand a cottage garden lot with a flowing spring, on the other an oppressive labyrinth with a brackish well.

Clifford and Hepzibah are essentially moon people, like Minerva and Mercury, people of the imagination and opponents to the empirical and grasping Pyncheons. Hepzibah, says McPherson, is also a complex mixture of the Gorgon figure, as protectress of Clifford, but an ineffectual one. The resolution of the action depends upon Phoebe and Holgrave, who typify their forebears in a new guise. Phoebe's sunniness is the Pyncheon sunniness in a new, feminine, domestic, gentle form; she is more like the Maules in her creativity, while Holgrave for his part softens the Maule artisan-wizardry traits with an intellectuality and love of art reminiscent of Alice Pyncheon. The cluster of imagery surrounding the tyrant father figure—sun, money, power, and flame—is integrated by the marriage of Phoebe and Holgrave with the moon, talent, wizardry, dream cluster that surrounds the Maules. Uncle Venner, who goes to live with them at the end, represents the benign aspect of the tyrant-father.

On the level of history, according to McPherson, the marriage symbolizes the attainment of mature independence. Maule's Well and the house of Pyncheon have merged together in the democratic unity of the descendants of the two lines, and the dream of eastern lands has become the reality of the new republic. The old house is abandoned for the new residence, which will last not for seven generations but for only one. While McPherson's interpretation of Hawthorne's mythic world may be too schematic, its complexities and symbolic richness, allied to that of Hawthorne's personal myth, add new density to our interpretation of *The House of the Seven Gables*.

RECENT INTERPRETATIONS

The 1970s gave rise to a variety of new critical methods, as mentioned above. Structuralism widens the areas of experience and culture in which literature is considered; reader response theory insists on the primacy of the readers' unmediated and subjective response to the text. In some criticism there is also a renewed sense of the market that the writer has to face to make a living. This form of criticism brings to bear the role economic forces and popular culture play in shaping literary texts. Finally, with a turn of the wheel of criticism, a new awareness of the religious tradition of New England has brought about a reexamination of the old question of Hawthorne's attitude toward Puritanism.

Some of these new approaches are used by Nina Baym in *The Shape of Hawthorne's Career* (1976), which is a careful reading of all of Hawthorne's significant texts. She claims that in his work there is a constantly changing attempt to define a way of writing "that could embody the imagination and justify it to a skeptical, practical-minded audience."[20]

The House of the Seven Gables, according to Baym, is similar in theme to *The Scarlet Letter*: there is a romantic conflict between the forces of passion, spontaneity, and creativity and the counterforces of regulation and control, represented respectively by the Maules and the Pyncheons. The Pyncheons symbolize the advent of civilization that replaces a creative and expressive relation to nature, as with the first Maule. At all times the Pyncheons resort to the law to dispossess or imprison others, even members of their own family, as can be seen in Jaffrey's treatment of Clifford. Such legalistic and grasping attitudes lead to the decay of the house.

Baym's analysis takes account of the social, psychological, and historical strands of the romance and focuses particularly on Holgrave as an artist figure who also represents fertility and sexuality. He is superior to his ancestral Maules in that he rejects witchcraft. He has escaped history even to the extent of taking on a new identity. Can he maintain this vitality and objectivity having returned to his roots?

Baym believes that Holgrave as Maule must assume some responsibility for Jaffrey's death. When he faces it, he does indeed change,
which we see in his new behavior toward Phoebe. This change, Baym
maintains, is caused not by his love for Phoebe, as has often been
claimed, but by his confrontation with death, which dispossesses Holgrave of the illusion of freedom. "At the end of the romance," Baym
writes, "he is a sad man" (Baym, 169). Holgrave does not get what he
wants, even though Hawthorne manipulates the ending so that it appears to be a happy one.

Baym says that this conflict in the ending is due to Hawthorne's
desire to write happy books: not because reader response influenced
him, since *The Scarlet Letter* had been well received by the public, but
because some inner censor directed him to be a writer of happy stories
and judged him lacking when he failed to do so.

A recent renewal of interest in the Puritan roots of American culture—perhaps a consequence of the current renewal of interest in religion at large—has also led to a reconsideration of Hawthorne's debt
to his Puritan ancestors. Sacvan Bercovitch in *The American Jeremiad*
(1978) has argued for the "richness, the complexity, and the continuing vitality, for good and ill, of American Puritan rhetoric"[21] and
points to the similarity of Hawthorne's fiction to the form of the jeremiad—the traditional lament and prophecy named after the fiery He-
brew prophet Jeremiah—which was a staple of Puritan preaching.
This turns our attention to what Whitman called "the problem of the
future of America." On the one hand, Hawthorne believed in America
as the promised land to come; on the other he ridiculed the notion. As
Bercovitch says, "It was as though he felt that for all the delusions of
American progressivism, no other mode of progress was available.
This is the moral . . . of the contrast he repeatedly makes between
rebellion and revolution . . . between Holgrave the anarchist who
wants to tear up society . . . and Holgrave the hero who joins the
consensus, marries a daughter of the Puritans, and transforms class-
conscious radicalism into suburban self-improvement" (Bercovitch,
206–7).

THE CONDITIONS OF INTERPRETATION

All of these interpretations, from Randall Stewart's orthodox Christian reading through the psychological, mythical, structural readings to Bercovitch's review of the Puritan heritage, can be seen, at least in part, to superimpose a particular set of critical presuppositions on Hawthorne's ambiguous and complex work, which many commentators in dozens of books and scores of articles have followed. To a degree, these readings can also be seen as reflections of the dominant thought patterns of the period. Every era reads Hawthorne in its own image, as indeed it reads any great author.

The early 1950s was an era of bland conformism and religious orthodoxy. Later on in that decade, when American studies began moving into the curriculum, there was a shift toward nationalism and myth and symbol making. The 1960s was a decade of unrest and revolt. Leslie Fiedler, reverting to D. H. Lawrence, who belonged to an earlier period of revolt, the 1920s, expresses the iconoclasm of the time. Freudianism, which also gained ground in the literary criticism of the 1920s, came back again in the 1960s to become a potent, if always contested, force in literary criticism.

Any comprehensive reading of *The House of the Seven Gables* must take account of all the forces working on Hawthorne's imagination—personal, social, political, religious, historical, psychological, formal, and traditional—as well as the needs of the market and the audience. Writing this novel was a complex balancing act for Hawthorne; and perhaps in trying to achieve many goals at once he took on too many. The richness and variety of the interpretations of the novel show that over a span of almost a century and a half it has challenged some of the best creative and critical minds of the time. It will no doubt continue to pose that challenge in the years to come.

A Reading

4

Personal Background and Sources

In writing *The House of the Seven Gables* Hawthorne drew from his own family and local history, his personal experience, as recorded in his notebooks, and his extensive reading to build a complex multilayered fiction. All the layers finally add up to a question of ultimate meaning that has bedevilled the critics since the book was first published more than 130 years ago. I would answer that the novel is a romance about the emancipation of a family from a hereditary curse, and, correspondingly, of a nation from the legacy of colonialism.

FAMILY HISTORY

The Hathorne family, as it was originally called, had been powerful and distinguished during the early years of settlement in New England. The first of them, William Hathorne, was a man of whom, in one respect at least, Hawthorne could be proud; he was the speaker in the Massachusetts House of Delegates and a major in the militia. On an issue of colonial authority he openly defied King Charles II, and he may have been a model for many of the colonial heroes that appear in Hawthorne's early historical tales.

Unfortunately there was another side of William Hathorne that for his great-great-grandson symbolized everything that was intolerant, cruel, proud, and vengeful in Puritanism. As a member of the General Court of Massachusetts, William was an arbiter of conduct and a moral advisor. He ran the police force and was a prosecutor who had a small army of informers who moved among the people. His duties included the detection and prosecution of carnal crimes, and he was excessively diligent in the punishment of such heinous offenses as kissing in public, dalliance, and unclean language. His punishments for minor crimes included having a man nailed by the ear to a pillory, which ear was later amputated. He caused a burglar to be branded with a "B" and also had his ear lopped off. A slave who was convicted of manslaughter was by Hathorne's recommendation burned at the stake.[1]

This tradition of interfering authority, vengeance, and cruelty was handed on untouched to William Hathorne's son, John. He was one of the three infamous judges at the Salem witchcraft trials. The event that lingered most in Hawthorne's imagination, and that seemed to him to lay a pall on all Hathorne posterity, was his ancestor's role in these trials of 1692 in which four hundred men and women were accused and twenty executed—"the most execrable scene," Nathaniel Hawthorne wrote in "Alice Doane's Appeal," "that our history blushes to record" (*Works*, 12:280).

A story was passed down through the Hawthorne family that one of the witches had pronounced a curse on Judge Hathorne and all his posterity, although in fact the curse was made against the Rev. Richard Noyes, another of the Salem judges. During these trials, John Hathorne and another judge caused John English and his wife to be arrested on charges of witchcraft. This led to continued bad feeling between the Hathornes and the Englishes over many years. This feud was patched up, however, when a grandson of Judge Hathorne married a great granddaughter of John English. Moreover, the English house, one of several that may have been used as a model for the House of the Seven Gables, passed into the possession of the Hathorne family. It stood, imposing, decaying, and empty for many years and was finally pulled down in 1833.

Personal Background and Sources

Later generations of Hathornes took to the sea. It is tempting to speculate that this was a psychological escape from a bloody family history. Hawthorne's father followed this sea-going custom. Captain Hathorne was a moody, solitary man, who, because he died when his son was only four, must have represented a distant, strange, romantic father figure to Hawthorne. On his mother's side, the Mannings, there had been a talent for business since the first family member migrated to New England in 1679. Hawthorne's uncle, Robert Manning, built up a large stagecoach line and was noted for growing and experimenting with fruit trees. The family moved to Maine when Hawthorne was twelve. There his uncles Robert and Richard owned a tract of land and had a claim on a much larger tract, a claim that was, however, never made good.

There was a less savory aspect to the Manning line. Hawthorne's maternal great-great-grandmother accused her husband, Thomas Manning, of committing incest with his own two sisters. He fled from town and did not reappear in Massachusetts for eight years. The sisters were convicted, fined, and forced to sit on stools in the center of the Salem meetinghouse with papers marked INCEST pinned to their caps.

This turbulent, lurid, and sensational Hathorne and Manning inheritance, as well as its now faded legacy of power, wealth, and influence, are all clearly evident in the narrative of *Seven Gables*. Hereditary guilt, hereditary pride, hereditary property, hereditary claims, hereditary decay, and the links between all five form the basis of the tale. In making the ancestral Colonel Pyncheon of *Seven Gables* the accuser and destroyer of Matthew Maule, Hawthorne recasts family history as a form of confession and expiation. He shrewdly links the accusation and condemnation of Maule to Pyncheon's coveting a piece of land owned by Maule on which he wishes to build his great new house. The stubborn Maule resists. When Maule is executed for witchcraft, Pyncheon acquires the desirable house plot, but the two families consequently come into conflict, a situation similar to the Hathorne-English family feud. Both the fictional and the historical feuds last until a marriage unites the clans.

Incest is a hidden theme in *Seven Gables*, because it was not a

31

subject that could be openly dealt with in the nineteenth-century American novel. For instance, comically and parodically, the incestuous Pyncheon chickens are openly compared to the family that has bred them. The possibility of incestuous relationships between Pyncheon family members is only vaguely hinted at in the novel, but Hawthorne supports this suggestion with his use of the antiquated custom of calling this long-established family "a house," aristocratic terminology that died out in postcolonial America. The decayed remnants of the House of Pyncheon cling to the decayed House of the Seven Gables in a comprehensive symbolic representation of inbreeding and lingering aristocratic pretension.

Hawthorne had an obsession with houses—possibly stemming from the days when his family could afford mansions—that is evident in all his fiction. His second book of stories was called *Mosses from the Old Manse* after the house where he lived in Concord; *Tanglewood Tales* was named after his house in the Berkshires. Each house was a source of inspiration and therefore was sacred to him. The "Custom-House" introduction records the place where he spent the years before writing *The Scarlet Letter;* its relaxed and friendly atmosphere balances the gloom of the house of Chillingworth and Dimmesdale. *The House of the Seven Gables* is thus not only an amalgam of family and historic houses in Salem, but the quintessential expression of all the symbolic and actual consequences of house ownership and hereditary transmission.

In his earlier work, Hawthorne made many sketches about houses that he would later draw on for the large canvas of his novel. As Julian Smith has pointed out, there are many similarities between Hawthorne's *Legends of the Province House*, written in the late 1830s, and *The House of the Seven Gables.*[2] The stories contrast a colonial, aristocratic past, rich in historical association and privilege, with a workaday, democratic present. In each, the old Province House in Boston, once the seat of government and in Hawthorne's day a decaying rooming house, is used to illustrate the difference between that storied past and the shabby present.

The Province House in the time of the Revolutionary War is made the scene of General Sir William Howe's great masquerade. Interrupting the feast comes a ghostly funeral procession of colonial governors that symbolizes the passing of the royal authority in New England. In "Edward Randolph's Portrait," a dark old picture hangs on the wall of the Province House. Randolph, an early governor of the colony, was responsible for a charter that gave the colonists almost democratic privileges. He later changed his attitude toward democracy and was subsequently detested as the destroyer of the liberties of New England.

The first of these two stories provides the model for the great feast with which Colonel Pyncheon opens his house for all his friends, and the second provides the model for the portrait on the wall of Pyncheon's house. The curse Edward Randolph earned by his acts against the people of colonial Massachusetts resembles the curse brought on the Pyncheon family by Colonel Pyncheon's sins against Matthew Maule.

The picture of the early royal governor, Edward Randolph, hangs on the wall of Province House, but it is so begrimed as to be invisible. A later royal governor, Thomas Hutchinson, is about to sign a paper calling out the troops against some discontented colonials when the figure of Randolph emerges from its covering of grime to warn him about the consequences. Hutchinson, however, ignores the warning and goes ahead with his tyrannical action. Later, dying in England, Hutchinson complains that he is choking with the blood of the Boston Massacre: he is killed by the burden of a people's curse. Again, there is a clear link to the Pyncheon curse.

The final Province House story, "Old Esther Dudley," is about an aristocratic old maid who stays alone in the house, haunting it like a ghost, after the British have been defeated in the Revolutionary War and General Howe has abandoned the house to return to England. Rumor has it that she summons from the mirror shades of past governors to keep her company; all are ghosts awaiting the day when a royal governor will return. The day dawns when she thinks that the governor has at last returned and she goes to greet him. She discovers, however, that the governor in question is the new governor of the state of Massachusetts, John Hancock. She calls him a traitor and sinks, dying, down on the floor. Hancock announces that he represents a new race of men, "living no longer in the past, scarcely in the present—but projecting our lives forward into the future. . . . Yet, let us reverence, for the last time, the stately and gorgeous prejudices of the tottering Past!" Esther Dudley dies, still swearing allegiance to the king; and the governor proclaims over her body, "We are no longer children of the Past!" (*Works*, 1:341). The similarities between Esther Dudley and Hepzibah are clear. Both hang on to an aristocratic and dead past; both represent the dangers of ancestral pride; both are links to a colonial aristocracy that is superseded by a democratic regime.

It is clear from all the Province House stories, however, that Hawthorne was not without ambivalence toward that colonial past. True, it is outmoded and superseded, but it retains a dignity and a sense of ceremony, honor, responsibility, and tradition that is lacking in the democratic present. In addition, Hawthorne, the romancer, takes pleasure in recording the splendid clothing, armor, and heraldry and in using the stately language of that past. All this ambivalence, he took into the writing of *The House of the Seven Gables*.

"Peter Goldthwaite's Treasure"

Another story of the same period, "Peter Goldthwaite's Treasure," is an even closer source for *The Seven Gables*. Old Peter is an impoverished businessman who has spent his life chasing a fortune by investing in illusory get-rich-quick schemes: gold prospecting, Mexican scrip, even lottery tickets. He has finally been reduced to penury; his only asset is the old gabled Goldthwaite house, which he has subbornly hung on to even though he has been offered a good price for it by a former business partner, John Brown. He lives on in the old house, tended by the aged housekeeper, Tabitha, who indulges him in his illusions. Peter's stubbornness is caused by his enduring belief in one surefire last resource—a legendary cache of wealth hidden somewhere in the fabric of the house by his great granduncle, also named Peter.

He spends a winter systematically gutting the house, until only the shell is left. Having reduced the house to one room, the kitchen, he at last finds an old chest. He eagerly opens it—only to find it full of old, worthless treasury notes, bills of land and banks—in fact, exactly the kind of speculative paper that Peter himself has invested in. It turns out that the great granduncle was identical to Peter in his ways; his life, too, was built on hope and illusion.

"Peter Goldthwaite's Treasure" is useful to Hawthorne, and may be useful to the reader of *The Seven Gables* in several ways. Goldthwaite's crumbling family house was an obvious source; Peter's mania to find the treasure trove is analogous, of course, to the Pyncheons' hereditary obsession with the deeds to the eastern lands. Peter's character also provides a draft for the impractical dreamer, Clifford. Peter shuts himself up in the house in order to tear it apart, but pausing in the destruction of an upper room, he throws open a window and finds a January thaw in progress. A lively parade of sledges and sleighs rushes by below him; bells jingle; laughter and shouts of pleasure fill the air. He catches a glimpse of how people keep themselves cheerful and prosperous through social pleasures and business, while he in seclusion pursues what might be a phantasm. "It is one great advantage of a gregarious mode of life," the narrator notes, "that each person rectifies his mind by other minds, and squares his conduct to that of his neighbors, so as seldom to be lost in eccentricity" (*Works*, 1:447).

Here is not only the seed to the chapter "The Arched Window" in *Seven Gables*, but also a clue to how both episodes are linked biographically to Hawthorne's own twelve-year seclusion, from which he was released by his courtship of Sophia. During his search of the upper room of the Goldthwaite house Peter also discovers sketches on a wall that he had made as a youth. One is of a ragged man with a spade leaning over to grasp something that he had found in a hole in the ground; behind him the devil is about the seize him. The sketch suggests the Faust myth: the treasure is to be purchased at the expense of the loss of the seeker's soul—which provides another interpretation of the Pyncheons' ancestral search for the deeds to the lost estate. But Peter is more like Clifford than Colonel or Jaffrey Pyncheon because there is an essential innocence and goodness in him that preserves his heart even in the midst of his obsession and isolation.

At the end of the story, John Brown, the practical businessman, turns up just as Peter is opening the chestful of worthless paper. As Holgrave rescues Clifford and Hepzibah, Brown rescues Peter and Tabitha and takes them to his house. The following day Peter will put the old house up for sale, and, he thinks, will apply for a guardian to take care of the proceeds to prevent him from embarking on more crazy schemes. So, as in *Seven Gables,* the past and the old house are left behind.

5

Literary Background:
The House of Many Meanings

Because of the themes he had developed in his earlier stories, Hawthorne carried authority and a great sureness of touch into the writing of his novel. But for the structure of his romance, as several critics have noted,[1] he went further back in time to the classical Greek dramatic trilogy by Aeschylus, *The Oresteia,* which tells part of the history of the House of Atreus. In that story the trouble starts when Thyestes seduces Atreus's wife. In revenge Atreus serves Thyestes a dish made of the flesh of his own children. When Thyestes finds out about this ghastly act, he curses the House of Atreus in perpetuity. Likewise, in *The House of the Seven Gables,* Maule curses the house of Pyncheon after Colonel Pyncheon has him condemned to death as a witch.

Atreus's sons, Agamemnon and Menelaus, respectively, marry Clytaemnestra and Helen. Cytaemnestra bears Agamemnon three children: Iphigenia, Electra, and Orestes. Paris of Troy seduces Menelaus's wife, Helen, and carries her off. To get her back, Agamemnon and Menelaus organize a great expedition against Troy, but the expedition is prevented from sailing by contrary winds. The prophet Calchas divines that this is due to the anger of the Gods. To appease the Gods,

Agamemnon sacrifices his daughter, Iphigenia. Similarly, in *The House of the Seven Gables* Gervase Pyncheon sacrifices his daughter Alice to obtain the deed to the great tract of land in Maine.

The cycle of revenge in the Greek tragedy continues with the murder of Agamemnon by Clytaemnestra, not only because of the sacrifice of their daughter, but also because Agamemnon has brought back a mistress, Cassandra, from Troy. Agamemnon's son, Orestes, revenges his father's death by killing his mother and her lover. This act is similar to the killing of Alice Pyncheon by Matthew Maule in *Seven Gables*. The cycle of revenge in *The Oresteia* is only ended by Orestes's trial and acquittal by an Athenian jury. At the end of *Seven Gables,* the curse is finally lifted by the marriage of the survivors of the two warring families.

Other literary houses are echoed in Hawthorne's novel. One predecessor is Spenser's House of Pride in book 1, canto 4 of *The Faerie Queen*. This is "A Stately Pallace built of squared brick, / . . . Full of faire windows, and delightfull bowres," but "all the hinder parts, that few could spie, / Were ruinous and old, but painted cunningly."[2]

John Bunyan's *The Pilgrim's Progress* is a more direct source.[3] In fact, so close are the analogies between the House of the Seven Gables and Bunyan's Interpreter's House that is clear that Hawthorne intended the book to be a modern, partly ironic, pilgrim's progress, a theory supported by other references in the text. Bunyan's hero, Christian, enters the Interpreter's House for guidance on his journey from the City of Destruction to the Celestial City. In the first room Christian sees a portrait of "a very grave person" on the wall, a crown of gold hanging over his head and a Bible in his hands. Compare this with the picture of Colonel Pyncheon, on the wall of the House of the Seven Gables. He is a stern Puritanical-looking personage, holding a Bible in one hand, but also "in the other uplifting an iron sword-hilt" (33). In the picture the sword stands out in far greater prominence than the Bible. In *The Pilgrim's Progress*, the picture depicts the man who will be Christian's guide on his difficult journey. By contrast, the Colonel is a false guide to the Pyncheons.

The Interpreter then leads Christian into another room that is full of dust. Here the Interpreter calls for a man to sweep and a maiden to sprinkle water to cleanse the room. Christian asks what this means. The Interpreter tells Christian that this room represents the heart of a man who was never sanctified by the grace of the Gospel; the dust is original sin and defiling corruptions. The sweeping man represents the Law and the sprinkled water the Gospel. There is a direct reference to this symbolism in Hawthorne's remark that the dusty old House of the Seven Gables "was itself like a great human heart, with a life of its own, and full of rich and sombre reminiscences" (27).

There are several other references to Bunyan's house in Hawthorne's house. The Interpreter shows Christian two allegorical figures in another room: one is Passion and the other is Patience. Judge Pyncheon's impatient greed represents Passion—which comes to nothing. Holgrave represents Patience—which waits and gets the prize in the end. The Interpreter says: "he . . . that hath his portion first, must needs have a time to spend it, but he that has his portion last must have it lastingly" (Bunyan, 63).

In yet another room is a man locked in an iron cage, which represents the sinner with the hardened heart. Again the analogy to Judge Pyncheon is clear: Hawthorne represents him again and again with images of iron. Christian asks the man in the iron cage what brought him there. The man replies: "For the lusts, pleasures, and profits of this world; in the enjoyment of which I did then promise myself much delight" (Bunyan, 67).

The last thing that Christian sees in the Interpreter's House before resuming his journey is a man getting out of bed, shaking and trembling. When asked why, the man replies that he has had a dream of Judgment Day in which the damned had been cast into a burning lake and the saved had been taken up into Heaven.

Hawthorne's text can be read as a secular version of Bunyan's Christian allegory—but it is of course partly ironic. The goal reached by Phoebe and Holgrave is married bliss, and for Hepzibah and Clifford the goal is material security and relief from oppression. But given the demands of the nineteenth-century audience with its limited patience for allegory, these rewards seem more appropriate than the Puritan rewards of Bunyan.

IS THERE A REAL HOUSE OF THE SEVEN GABLES?

Naturally, Hawthorne's novel cast a long shadow over its place of origin, Salem, Massachusetts. Several houses have been named as the origin of the House of the Seven Gables. In *Hawthorne's Country,* Helen Archibald Clarke mentions some of the pretenders.[4] One was the now vanished English house; another was known as the Curwen mansion, but the chief pretender was a house of many gables on Turner Street, near the Salem Bay. This house belonged to Hawthorne's cousin, Miss Ingersoll. According to Clarke, local tradition holds that Hawthorne spent many hours in this house and was told that it originally had seven gables, although the number had subsequently been reduced to five. Hawthorne seemed infatuated by the sound of the name, "house of the seven gables." He told his cousin: "It is just what I wanted" (Clarke, 149).

Early in the twentieth century an enterprising woman saw the opportunity and bought the Ingersoll house. She consulted an architect who went to work and discovered several beams where the old gables ought to have been and restored the house to its supposed original condition. An old oaken door, studded with nails, was found in the attic and became the model for a restored front door for the house; the kitchen was restored to its mid–nineteenth-century condition, complete with a large brick fireplace, with an old-fashioned iron oven in which bread can be baked. Nearby is kept a toasting fork that is reputed to be the one that Hawthorne's cousin Ingersoll used to toast bread for him. The cent-shop was also "restored" to its supposed original condition, complete with the jangling bell to announce customers. On completion, the house was turned into a museum. Tourists could pay their money, take a tour, and eat Jim Crow gingerbread, just as Hepzibah's first customer, the little boy, did.

Henry James, for one, was not fooled by this Hawthorne museum. When he made a pilgrimage to Salem in 1906 to seek out the remnants of Hawthorne's life there, he was sadly disappointed by the place. He wrote:

The weak, vague domiciliary presence at the end of the lane may have "been" . . . the idea of the admirable book—though even here we take a leap into dense darkness; but the idea that it is the inner force of the admirable book so vividly forgets, before our eyes, any such origin or reference, "cutting" it dead as a low acquaintance and outsoaring the shadow of its night, that the connection has turned a somersault into space, repudiated like a ladder kicked back from the top of a wall. Hawthorne's ladder at Salem, in fine, has now quite gone. . . .[5]

James ruefully recognized that genius is elusive and that we are condemned to know it only after the fact. The house was totally the creation of Hawthorne's mind, even though it may have had one, or several, prototypes. He created the house out of a general style of colonial architecture, examples of which could still be seen in Salem when he was young.

6

Gothic Romance and the Plot

While reading *The House of the Seven Gables* we are conscious much of the time that we are reading not a realistic narrative, but one shot through with the moonbeams and marvels of romance. Hawthorne drew much of his inspiration for his romance from the Gothic romance tradition, which has its roots in eighteenth-century English literature. Some have speculated that this literary genre represents a revolt against, on the one hand, the excessive rationality of eighteenth-century literature, as practiced by Alexander Pope, Jonathan Swift, Dr. Johnson, and many others, and on the other, the sentimental novel, as practiced by Samuel Richardson and his followers. Certainly Gothic romance delved into the underside of the rational mind: the world of dreams, spirits, fear, and evil.

Robert Walpole's *The Castle of Otranto* (1765) was the forerunner of most Gothic romances and created the conventions that are adhered to in such classics in the genre as Mrs. Radcliffe's *The Mysteries of Udolpho* (1794), William Godwin's *Caleb Williams* (1794), M. G. Lewis's *The Monk* (1796), and Charles Robert Maturin's *Melmoth the Wanderer* (1820). The "machinery" of these novels generally includes a gloomy haunted castle or house, with drafty corridors and labyrinthine subterranean passages that often contain a secret cabinet or two. At the center of the Gothic plot is a mysterious crime, usually perpetrated by the hero-villain and often in the form of the undoing of a fair and innocent maiden, or an incestuous relationship. This villain, too, often has magic powers. He inevitably meets a bad end and leaves, shrieking, destined for hell. There are mysterious portraits that often come to life, mirrors that show the truth or the future, strange music, living dead, ghosts and spirits (real or fake), ghostly footsteps, rattling chains and creaking doors. There are quite often quantities of blood, which emanates from the nostrils and mouths of the living or the dead. Nature contributes to the picture with storms at appropriate moments, deep darkness, and, often, the pale glimmer of the moon. Finally, there is usually some deus ex machina who appears at the end to reward virtue and punish evil. Much of this machinery has survived up to the present day into countless Hollywood or television horror flicks. Then as now, much of this fiction is sensational and titillating, feeding on mankind's desire to be shocked, surprised, and scared, and serves as a form of release from the daily round of reality.

In crossing the Atlantic, the Gothic romance underwent a sea change at the hands of masters like Edgar Allan Poe and Nathaniel Hawthorne. While employing the machinery to good effect, these authors also created a psychological and symbolic dimension usually missing from the English versions of Gothic. In "The Fall of the House of Usher" Poe uses the decaying ancestral house of the family as an analogue to the mind of Roderick Usher. Usher points to the symbiotic relationship between the miasmatic, decaying old house and his fear, depression, encroaching insanity, and physical decay. His decline is hastened by the death of his twin sister, Madeline, from some unknown malady.

In one of those grand melodramatic climaxes for which Poe is famous, Madeline escapes from her sealed and barred tomb, into which she has apparently been placed still living. Her white burial garments covered in blood, she throws herself on her brother, and bears him to the floor as they are both dying. As the appalled narrator flees, the house collapses behind him into the dark water of the surrounding tarn.

Roderick has told the narrator before the final appearance of his sister that he has known for days that she is not dead. He does not say why he has not gone down to the tomb to release her. The only possible inference is that he is paralyzed with guilt over an incestuous relationship with his sister and he hopes he has buried the secret knowledge with her. But the body of his sister and the guilt combine to destroy him.

Hawthorne uses all these elements of English and American Gothic in writing *The House of the Seven Gables*. The devices are sometimes transparent, as in the use of the ancestral portrait. Hawthorne is always careful, however, to hedge his use of the Gothic supernatural with ambiguity so the portrait only "seems" to "symbolize an evil influence" on the house (21), just as the mirror in another room of the house "was fabled" to contain within its depths all the shapes of the generations of the Pyncheon family who had gazed into it (20). Often, like Jane Austen in *Northanger Abbey*, Hawthorne parodies the Gothic conventions, as when the ghostly footsteps and spectral presence much heralded in chapter 7 turn out to be the "material ghost" of Clifford (105).

The most obvious example of the influence of Gothic romance in *Seven Gables* is the chapter "Alice Pyncheon," in which Holgrave tells Phoebe the story of Alice. This story within the story is distanced from the realistic narrative of the novel. Gervase Pyncheon, the Colonel's son, has lived long in England and hopes to go back there wealthy so that he can solicit or purchase an earldom and also gain for his daughter, Alice, marriage to an English duke or German prince. To this end Gervase tries to persuade Matthew Maule to reveal to him the whereabouts of the deeds to the fabled lands in Maine. Faustian greed combines with wizardry to impel Gervase to sacrifice Alice to gain his end.

This legend comes with all the appropriate Gothic trappings: the portrait on the wall frowns and shakes its fist at the proceedings. Maule becomes the evil villain who entraps the virgin heroine by his hypnotic power and then bewitches her so that from that time forth she is a slave to his every wish.

Gothic Romance and the Plot

As William Bysshe Stein has pointed out in *Hawthorne's Faust,* there is a strong strain of the Faust myth in Gothic romance.[1] The hero-villain gains power over other mortals through some kind of compact or alliance with mystical powers. This compact is at the center of many Gothic plots. Hawthorne was particularly attracted to this aspect of the tradition, as can also be seen in the figure of Chillingworth in *The Scarlet Letter.* Matthew Maule is another Faustian figure, for he essentially trades his humanity for his hypnotic power over Alice Pyncheon.

The most significant aspect of "Alice Pyncheon," however, is Hawthorne's treatment of its narrator, Holgrave. The dramatic telling of the tale by the young author induces in his audience, Phoebe, a hypnotic state similar to that induced in Alice Pyncheon by Matthew Maule. But Holgrave, unlike his ancestor, resists the Faustian temptation to gain power over Phoebe. He has what Hawthorne calls "the rare and high quality of reverence for another's individuality" (212), and he releases Phoebe from the spell. In so doing he proves different from all the other artist-scientist figures in Hawthorne's work—Chillingworth, Ethan Brand, Owen Warland in "The Artist of the Beautiful," Dr. Rappaccini in "Rappaccini's Daughter," and Aylmer in "The Birthmark." All of them are finally damned by the use of their powers, whereas Holgrave is saved by his refusal to use his power over Phoebe to violate the sanctity of her heart. This refusal to act puts him in train for the happy outcome of the story.

Essentially, Hawthorne has parodied the Gothic romance tradition in *The House of the Seven Gables.* Within the realistic framework of the novel, it becomes a kind of comic element: instead of the traditional door, it is the machinery that creaks; the ghost turns out to be human; the magical powers are renounced; the aristocratic foundation of the romance is made to look absurd and outmoded; and a light-filled democratic realism takes over from a dusky, pestiferous past.

7

History and Modernity

Among many other things, *Seven Gables* is a novel about history, a meditation on the effects of New England's colonial and Puritan past on the nineteenth-century present. As F. O. Matthiessen has pointed out, "Looking back over the whole history of his province, [Hawthorne] was more struck by decay than by potentiality, by the broken ends to which the Puritan effort had finally come."[1] The weight of the past was heavy indeed for Hawthorne. He was encumbered not only by the economic, political, and religious history of his town, but also by the part played by his family in such a history. He was acutely aware of the fallen fortunes of the Hathorne's, and contrasted his own lot, as a struggling writer, with the wealth and influence that his family had once wielded in the town. His low social status seems to have troubled him; and there is often an edge to his satire on his native town. He could look back on the past as a time of power for his family, even when that power was abused. The present, by contrast, often seemed impalpable to him.

THE INFLUENCE OF THE PAST

Particularly in the decaying port of Salem, the past had a greater sway than anywhere else in America. The cobbled streets, the civic buildings, the old port, the houses, many of them decaying and shabby, all spoke to him eloquently of a past that lived on into the present and shaped it. James Russell Lowell, the eminent New England poet and historian, wrote to tell Hawthorne that *The House of the Seven Gables* was "the most valuable contribution to New England history that has been made," because it deals with the connection between ancestry and descent, "which historians so carefully overlook. Yesterday is commonly looked upon and written about as of no kin to To-day, though the one is legitimate child of the other, and has its veins filled with the same blood."[2] Similarly, Henry James noted Hawthorne's capacity to create in his romance "the interest *behind* the interest of things, as continuous with the very life we are leading . . . round about him and under his eyes." This made *Seven Gables* a singularly happy example of "the real as distinguished from the artificial romantic note."[3] Unlike conventional writers of historical romance, Hawthorne does not simply take a slice of the past, dress it up in the appropriate historical costume and furnishings, and represent it as a complete and hermetic whole. He sees the past as having both an intrinsic interest and importance and a relevant moral and social influence on the present.

The introductory chapter of *Seven Gables*, in which Hawthorne sketches the colonial past of the town, and the many other passages referring to that past elsewhere in the book are some of the most memorable of all. The descendants of the old colonial aristocracy continue to have influence long after their energy and moral influence have withered. Resistance to the democratic impulse, as represented by the daguerreotypist Holgrave, is correspondingly strong.

COLONIAL ROOTS

The corruption of colonial power is an enduring theme in Hawthorne's work that goes back to an early story, "The Gray Champion," first published in 1835. The story takes place in 1688: the Massachusetts colonial governor, Sir Edmund Andros, taking his mandate from King Charles II, has denied freedom of the press, violated civil rights, passed laws and levied taxes without the consent of the governed, and enforced his rule with military power. The people assemble in the streets prepared to do battle for their rights, and the governor's soldiers advance on them, in a march that is, Hawthorne writes, "like the progress of a machine" (*Works*, 1:25). The machine is stopped not by the people, however, but by an aged, proud Puritan who advances on them alone. One of the governor's officers says, laughingly: "See you not, he is some old round-headed dignitary, who hath lain asleep these thirty years, and knows nothing of the change of times? Doubtless, he thinks to put us down with a proclamation in Old Noll's [Cromwell's] name!" (*Works*, 1:29). The joke, however, is on the governor's men: the Gray Champion *is* a ghost from the past, "the type of New England's hereditary spirit" that appears whenever "the invader's step pollutes the soil" (*Works*, 1:31). The Champion warns the governor that his power has ended; "the Popish tyrant" (*Works*, 1:29) in England has been deposed. For in the year of the Glorious Revolution, 1688, the Protestant William of Orange was installed on the throne of England, ending the reign of the Catholic Stuarts.

In "The Gray Champion" the image of the machine advancing on the colonials represents not only armed force but also arbitrary colonial power. The machine is halted by the old Champion who restores to the citizens of Massachusetts the hereditary rights claimed by the first settlers who left England to escape the arbitrary rule of church and state. Yet that arbitrary power is always ready to reassert itself. Hawthorne claims that the Gray Champion appeared again in the revolutionary period at Lexington and at Bunker Hill, when the colonists once more took up arms against the king's power. Even after independence, colonial power lingers on in the shape of families like the Pyncheons who emulate their aristocratic forebears in trying to expand their wealth and power at the expense of their weaker and poorer brethren.

Hawthorne creates the image of this colonial power in the House of the Seven Gables in that it has been the home for successive generations of Pyncheons, who, however, with a few exceptions, had become increasingly impoverished. Its decay is evident in its fabric and its overgrown garden. One Pyncheon in the mid-eighteenth century, reduced to penury, had cut a shop door into the side of the house and subsided into trade. It is said that his ghost can be seen at night, poring over his ledger, a look of "unutterable woe upon his face" so that it was "his doom to spend eternity in a vain effort to make his accounts balance" (29).

REALISM, SYMBOLISM, AND ALLEGORY

Nearly everything in and around the house, it seems, works on at least two levels—realism and symbolism—and sometimes on a third level, of allegory. The symbol establishes a second level of meaning, the allegory a second level of story. Hawthorne spends a great deal of his time describing the house, aiming at the kind of fidelity achieved in seventeenth-century Dutch paintings of domestic scenes. In a tale of ancient wrong, witchcraft, hauntings, and fate it is particularly important for him to provide a solid anchor in reality, just as Melville does in the cetology chapters—the long descriptions of whaling practices—of *Moby-Dick*. The feast that is supposed to inaugurate the house is described with fidelity, again reminiscent of Dutch still lifes. With equal care Hawthorne describes the contents of Hepzibah's cent-shop. In describing the garden, Hawthorne allows his fancy freer rein. When the little country cousin, Phoebe, first visits the garden, she finds that its disorder has been partly set to rights by the daguerreotypist, Holgrave, so that it is now producing vegetables, fruit, and flowers. But there is also a fountain that appears to produce "a continually shifting apparition of quaint figures, vanishing too suddenly to be definable" (88)—an emblem of the more fanciful parts of the novel. This is Maule's Well, cursed since the building of the house.

Hawthorne's imaginary house is built on the spot first covered by Maule's log hut, thus, as some hint at the time, "over an unquiet grave" (9). It thus embodies that house of nature within its brick and stone and mortar. Maule had built his house there because of a singularly pure spring. When Pyncheon built his house, the water in Maule's Well, as it was called, turned hard and brackish. The symbolism is clear: the Edenic purity of the early garden has been destroyed by Pyncheon's crime; the polluted spring is the emblem both of a fallen world and of the creation of an unjust colonial power structure. The apparently realistic chickens that roam the garden, descendants of an ancient breed, also become emblematic. Once a large size, the breed has now become "scarcely larger than pigeons, and had a queer, rusty, withered aspect" (88). Like many a noble race, Hawthorne adds, they have degenerated, "in consequence of too strict a watchfulness to keep it pure" (89), hinting, here, at incest. Since he presses the analogy between the coop of chickens and the house of Pyncheons—who are "somehow mixed up in its destiny" (89)—there is more than a hint of incest in the Pyncheon clan too, which at least in part explains its weakness and degeneracy. Phoebe is largely exempt from this taint because she is the child of a Pyncheon who married into a working-class family, thus bringing new blood into a tired race.

Two central allegorical threads run through *The House of the Seven Gables*. The first, alluded to many times throughout the narrative, is the story of the Garden of Eden and man's original sin, his fall from paradise, and the possibility of redemption. The second, already discussed, is drawn from Bunyan's progress of the pilgrim toward the Celestial City. These allegories are, of course, closely linked. Throughout most of the story the house represents the fallen world, yet it is the only world that the Pyncheons know. Clifford and Hepzibah try to flee from it to embark on their journey of salvation after the death of Judge Pyncheon, yet they are drawn irrevocably back and cannot escape until the curse has been experienced and lifted by Holgrave and Phoebe.

The house also represents the body and the worldly experience of man, which the soul must leave in order to be free. Hawthorne describes the house graphically in the first chapter, "The Old Pyncheon Family." "So much of mankind's varied experience had passed there," he writes,"—so much had been suffered, and something, too, enjoyed—that the very timbers were oozy, as with the moisture of a heart" (27). Another level of allegory is alluded to throughout the narrative. The aristocratic house of Pyncheon represents a colonial past, the attachment to the king and to a hereditary order. The plebeian Maules represent an independent, democratic nation, suppressed and dispossessed by colonial power. The revolution of 1776, it is true, ended with the independence of the United States, but Hawthorne in *Seven Gables* is talking about other kinds of psychological and cultural dependence. It is necessary for Americans, he is saying, to throw off this "dead hand of the past," to leave the decaying aristocratic mansion of the Pyncheons for the wooden-built, and therefore far more easily destroyed and renewed, houses of a democratic present. The biblical saying, "Sufficient unto the day is the evil thereof" (Matt. 6:34), is the implicit motto of *The House of the Seven Gables*. On all levels of realism, symbolism, and allegory, the novel is all about the possibility of change and renewal.

Given this weight of the past, it was not easy for Hawthorne to tip the scale of the novel in favor of the present, as he obviously intended to do at the conclusion. We feel that the decaying structure of the House of the Seven Gables is still far from tumbling down. Colonial history and legend and the trappings of romance are the mainspring to the plot of *The House of the Seven Gables*.

THE IMPACT OF HAWTHORNE'S TIME

Hawthorne then had to bring to bear as a counterweight the daylight reality of the science and technology of the nineteenth century. A large part of this burden rests on the rather slender shoulders of Holgrave; his occupation as daguerreotypist is one symbol of this process. This version of the photographic method was invented in 1839—twelve years before the publication of *The House of the Seven Gables*. Louis-Jacques-Mandé Daguerre, the inventor of the process, shot to instantaneous fame, gave weekly demonstrations to fascinated audiences in Paris, and published a manual, *A History and Description of the Process of Daguerreotype*, which went into twenty-six editions in various countries before the end of 1839. The process caught on faster in the United States—a country perennially fascinated by new technology—than anywhere else. Travelling daguerreotypists, like Holgrave, fanned out all over the country from centers where it was first introduced—Philadelphia, New York, and Boston.

The process brought a rapid change to the contemporary perception of reality. For the first time there was no human intervention between the natural object or the human form and its representation. The photographer was in fact more an artisan than an artist, serving a mechanical process that reproduced nature and man exactly as it was defined by the camera lens, albeit in monotone.

Nothing could be further from the process of the Gothic romancer—who embellishes and exaggerates almost every aspect of man and nature—than daguerreotype. Hawthorne had a glimmering of how photography would change the nature of art. This is shown particularly in the passage in which Holgrave shows the daguerreotype of Judge Pyncheon to Phoebe. He points out that the sun operating on the photographic plate "actually brings out the secret character with a truth that no painter would ever venture upon, even could he detect it" (91). Although Pyncheon shows to the world "an exceedingly pleasant countenance, indicative of benevolence, openness of heart, sunny good humor, and other praiseworthy qualities of that cast," the sun tells quite another story. It reveals the real man, "sly, subtle, hard, imperious, and, withal, cold as ice" (92). There can be no escaping from the truth of this process—a scientific, direct imitation of nature—whereas painters, skilled as they might be, can be fooled by appearances, or perhaps persuaded by power and wealth, they will conceal or embellish reality.

The other major technological development of the mid-nineteenth century was the construction of railways. The first passenger and freight line for steam locomotives was built in England between Stockton and Darlington in 1825. George Stephenson built his famous locomotive "The Rocket" for the Liverpool to Manchester Railway in 1829. Soon after that the first lines were built in the United States. After 1830 the railroads grew so quickly that by 1840 the total number of miles of railroad tracks outnumbered that of the canals. Hawthorne was fascinated by this new mode of transportation. He wrote about it first in the amusing tale "The Celestial Railroad" (1843), which is an update and parody of Bunyan's *The Pilgrim's Progress*. The dreamer-narrator discovers that some of the inhabitants of the City of Destruction have vastly improved communications between their city and the Celestial City by building a railroad between them. This capitalistic enterprise is designed to shorten the trip to the Celestial City and make it far more comfortable than it was by the old long and perilous footpath. Mr. Smooth-it-away, Mr. Live-for-the-world, and other characters from Bunyan assure the narrator of the benefits of this new mode of transportation, so he is surprised to see from the train window two pilgrims toiling over the old rocky path. It turns out that the driver of the train is none other than Christian's old adversary, Apollyon, and the locomotive is "much more like a sort of mechanical demon that would hurry us to the infernal region than a laudable contrivance for smoothing our way to the Celestial City" (*Works*, 2:216). The narrator thankfully awakens from the dream just before he reaches that hellish destination.

It is clear from this story that Hawthorne looked upon the railroad with a certain ambivalence, as did his former neighbor in Concord, Henry David Thoreau. Watching the freight and passenger trains go by not far from his hut on Walden Pond, in *Walden* (1854) Thoreau revels in the power and energy of this mechanical horse, and speculates that the earth has at last got a race worthy to inhabit it. But then he laments: "If all were as it seems, and men made the elements their servants for noble ends! If the cloud that hangs over the engine were the perspiration of heroic deeds, or as beneficent as that which floats over the farmer's field, then the elements and Nature herself would cheerfully accompany men on their errands and be their escort." Concluding, however, that, useful as it is for commerce, the railroad is destroying pastoral life; Thoreau decides as far as possible to avoid it. "I will not," he declares, "have my eyes put out and my ears spoiled by its smoke and steam and hissing."[4]

Leo Marx has analyzed the phenomenon of industrialization and its impact on literary sensibility in his *The Machine in the Garden: Technology and the Pastoral Ideal in America* (1964).[5] The tension between the pastoral ideal and the onset of technology was at its greatest, Marx says, between 1840 and 1860. *The House of the Seven Gables* was written squarely in the middle of this period. Marx continues, "The locomotive, associated with fire, smoke, speed, iron, and noise, is the leading symbol of the new industrial power. It appears in the woods, suddenly shattering the harmony of the green hollow, like a presentiment of history bearing down on the American asylum" (Marx, 27). Again and again, American writers of the period depict the machine as intruding on an enclosed space, a shocking invader of a fantasy of idyllic satisfaction. "It invariably is associated with crude, masculine aggressiveness," Marx asserts, "in contrast with the tender, feminine, and submissive attitudes traditionally attached to the landscape" (Marx, 29).

It is fitting, then, that the pilgrimage, as Hawthorne calls it, that Hepzibah and Clifford take when fleeing from the House of the Seven Gables and the body of Judge Pyncheon takes the form of a railway journey. The reader gets a vivid sense of what this new mode of travel meant to the nineteenth-century mind. To those used to the immemorial movement of the horse-drawn vehicle, railway travel was a distinct dislocation of sensibilities.

The world races past the travelers. "The spires of meetinghouses," the narrator notes, "seemed set adrift from their foundations; the broad-based hills glided away. Everything was unfixed from its age-long rest, and moving at whirlwind speed in a direction opposite to their own" (256). Technology for Hawthorne, as for Charles Dickens and many other Victorians in the industrial age, seemed to be challenging the institutions of religion and even the solid hills, "from whence," as the psalmist sang, "cometh our help." It must also be remembered that this mode of travel was at that time accompanied by considerable noise, both from the rolling stock and the locomotive, and by the smell of smoke and the nuisance of ash. It was also not without danger, as contemporary reports of many railroad accidents attest.

Clifford, however, is enthralled by this new mode of transportation, calling it "positively the greatest blessing that the ages have wrought out for us." Annihilating "the toil and dust of pilgrimage," Clifford adds, the trains "spiritualize travel!" (260). Why, then, should anyone, Clifford asks, be made a prisoner of bricks and stone when he can dwell anywhere? From this, the wildly enthusiastic Clifford goes on to a long condemnation of settled habitation, and real estate itself, and to an encomium of other wonders of modern science: mesmerism and electricity. His fellow traveler to whom he is pouring out this praise to technology observes that the electric telegraph is most useful in detecting bank robbers and murderers, but Clifford scorns this misuse of technology and says the telegraph should be consecrated to "high, deep, joyful and holy missions," to send messages of love and remembrance (264–65).

Hawthorne's ambivalence to the railroad is made clear by the variety of comments that he makes about it. On the one hand there is the reference to the whirling away of meetinghouses and the hills themselves; on the other he can see that the railroad as an emblem of progress, a means by which the various conditions and classes of humanity can mix and communicate, shake loose the stranglehold of the past, and serve democratic ends. "New people continually entered [the train]," he writes. "Old acquaintances—for such they soon grew to be, in this rapid current of affairs—continually departed. Here and there, amid the rumble and the tumult, sat one asleep. Sleep; sport; business; graver or lighter study;—and the common and inevitable movement onward! It was life itself!" (257).

The railroad and the telegraph between them were rapidly annihilating distance and time, increasing commerce, hastening change, and loosening the close-knit social fabric of villages and towns throughout America. The feverish paean of praise that Clifford gives to these emblems of progress is the consequence of a sudden access of masculine decisiveness and power in the surge of his relief at the death of his tormentor, Judge Pyncheon. Soon enough, however, his essentially feminine, submissive nature reasserts itself. In utter weakness and lassitude, he and Hepzibah descend to a wayside station near a ruined church and farmhouse. These ruins would seem to be symbols first of the decline of the power of the church and religion and second of increasing urbanization and the decline of agriculture. In spite of these symbolic ruins, the only thing that the distraught Hepzibah can think to do is sink to her knees: "no juncture this," comments the narrator, "to question that there was a sky above, and an Almighty Father looking down from it!" (267). The cost of technology for this generation seems to have been a high one, spiritually speaking. The stranded pair, however, can only fall back on prayers to the old God, the Father, and ask his mercy.

8

Happy Endings?

We know from letters and other sources that Hawthorne's desires to find a larger audience and the urgings of his wife, Sophia, drove him to writing a sunnier tale than the dark imaginings of his previous novel, *The Scarlet Letter*. His endeavors certainly pleased his wife. She wrote to a friend on 27 January 1851: "'The House of the Seven Gables' was finished yesterday. Mr. Hawthorne read me the close last evening. There is an unspeakable grace and beauty in the conclusion, throwing back upon the sterner tragedy of the commencement an ethereal light, and a dear home-loveliness and satisfaction. How you will enjoy the book,—its depth of wisdom, its high tone, the flowers of Paradise scattered over all the dark places."[1] The cloying, sentimental note of this letter supports the argument that Hawthorne was aiming to please not only his wife but also popular taste when he wrote *The House of the Seven Gables*. The evidence for this taste can best be found in the romantic fiction that appeared in the contemporary magazines—magazines for which Hawthorne had also written a number of tales.

Whatever the motive, Hawthorne wished to provide a happy resolution to an ancient wrong and made conscious efforts to lighten the book after the grim chapter on the death of Judge Pyncheon. Did he succeed in this endeavor? As we saw from comments quoted earlier, Evert Duyckinck did not think so. In a reply to Duyckinck's review, Hawthorne wrote:

> It appears to me that you like the book better than the Scarlet Letter; and I certainly think it a more natural and healthy product of my mind, and felt less reluctance in publishing it. I cannot quite understand why everything that I write takes so melancholy an aspect in your eyes. As regards this particular story, I really had an idea that it was rather a cheerful one than otherwise; but, in writing it, I suppose I was illuminated by my purpose to bring it to a prosperous close; while the gloom of the past threw its shadow along the reader's pathway. (*Letters*, 16:421)

The letter that Melville wrote Hawthorne after reading *The House of the Seven Gables* stands in stark contrast to the one written by Mrs. Hawthorne and is one of the most remarkable in all literary history. It is worth quoting at length because of its revelation of the darkness that this sympathetic reader saw in the novel. After praising the richness and abundance of the novel, with its "admirable sideboard, plentifully stored with good viands," and its "smell of old wine in the pantry," Melville wrote:

> and finally, in one corner, there is a dark little black-letter volume in golden clasps, entitled "Hawthorne: A Problem." It has delighted us; it has piqued a re-perusal; it has robbed us of a day, and made us a present of a whole year of thoughtfulness; it has bred great exhilaration and exultation with the remembrance that the architect of the Gables resides only six miles off, and not three thousand miles away, in England, say. . . . The curtains are more drawn; the sun comes in more; genialities peep out more. . . . And here we would say that, did circumstances permit, we should like nothing better than to devote an elaborate and careful paper to the full consideration and analysis of the purport and significance of what so strongly characterizes all of this author's writings. There is a certain tragic phase of humanity which, in our opinion, was never more powerfully embodied than by Hawthorne. We mean the tragedies

of human thought in its own unbiassed, native, and profounder
workings. We think that into no recorded mind has the intense feeling of the usable truth ever entered more deeply than into this
man's. By usable truth, we mean the apprehension of the absolute
condition of present things as they strike the eye of man who fears
them not, though they do their worst in him. . . .

There is the grand truth about Nathaniel Hawthorne. He says
NO! in thunder; but the devil himself cannot make him say *yes*. For
all men who say *yes*, lie; and all men who say *no*,—why, they are
in the happy condition of judicious, unincumbered travellers in Europe; they cross the frontiers into Eternity with nothing but a carpet
bag,—that is to say, the Ego.[2]

Melville is clearly referring back to *The Scarlet Letter* when he mentions the sun peeping out more in *The House of the Seven Gables*. But
he is not taken in by the sunny aspect of the later novel. He sees in it
a problem just like that of the previous novel—and surely the problem
is evil and its power to dominate human life even through subsequent
generations. This must be "the usable truth" that Melville talks about,
"the absolute condition of present things" that manifests itself in all
of Hawthorne's work, no matter how much cheerfulness or happiness
or glimpses of Eden he puts in his fiction. All the sentimental ladies of
the popular magazines can pen their little affirmations of romantic
love till the cows come home, but Hawthorne, although appearing to
write in that vein is, Melville sees, still saying "NO" in thunder, like
the prophets of the Old Testament; and no manner of affirmatives and
good wishes will change that. Unencumbered, like Christian in *The
Pilgrim's Progress*, Hawthorne travels through the valley of the
shadow.

No doubt the major source of dark shadows in *The House of the
Seven Gables* is Hawthorne's immersion in the Calvinistic doctrines of
original sin. As Melville had discerningly written in an earlier review
of *Mosses from An Old Manse*, "Certain it is . . . that this great power
of blackness in him derives its force from its appeals to that Calvinistic
sense of Innate Depravity and Original Sin, from whose visitations, in
some shape or other, no deeply thinking mind is always and wholly
free. For, in certain moods, no man can weigh this world, without

throwing in something, somehow like Original Sin, to strike the uneven balance"[3] Melville would seem to have been forecasting Hawthorne's attempts to write a sunny book in *The House of the Seven Gables*, when he continues, "At all events, perhaps no writer has ever wielded this terrific thought with greater terror than this same harmless Hawthorne. Still more: this black conceit pervades him, through and through. You may be witched by his sunlight,—transported by the bright gildings in the skies he builds over you;—but there is the blackness of darkness beyond; and even his bright gildings but fringe and play upon the edges of thunder clouds" (Melville, 9:243). Hawthorne never had a better reader than Melville, who became his friend soon after this piece was written. Melville was the first to recognize the cosmic joke that Hawthorne was playing on his readers—presenting on the face of things a world of kindness and sunniness, which is really a thin skin over the endemic deviltry of man and nature.

9

The Bible

Hawthorne found warrant for his view of the world in the Old and New Testaments, which he knew intimately. The Old Testament, however, figures far more prominently than the New in *The House of the Seven Gables*. The act that sets the plot in motion, the false accusation by Colonel Pyncheon against Matthew Maule in order to gain his plot of land, is modeled on Ahab's plot to gain Naboth's vineyard through false accusation. Like Naboth, Maule is condemned to death. The house of Ahab, like the house of Pyncheon, is cursed through the generations (1 Kings 21,22). Maule's curse on Colonel Pyncheon also relates to God's promise to Moses in the Book of Numbers to visit "the iniquity of the fathers upon the children unto the third and fourth generation" (Num. 14: 18). Maule cries to Colonel Pyncheon: "God will give him blood to drink" (8). The biblical source of this curse is in the Book of Revelation in which the prophet talks of the seven angels and the seven last plagues of the wrath of God. The third angel "poured out his vial of wrath upon the rivers and fountains of waters, and they became blood." The angel declares, "they have shed the blood of saints and prophets, and thou hast given them blood to drink" (Rev. 16: 4–6). The importance of blood for atonement is seen throughout the Old Testament and is transformed in the New Testament into the ceremony of Eucharist. "For the Life of the Flesh," the Lord says in Leviticus, "is in the blood: and I have given it to you upon the altar to make an atonement for your souls: for it is the blood that maketh an atonement for the soul" (Lev. 17: 11).

THE SEVEN DEADLY SINS

The mystical number 7 is reminiscent of not only the seven angels of Revelation and all the other sevens of that book—the candlesticks, stars, churches, and seals—but also the seven deadly sins. Evert Duyckinck was the first to point out the connection between the seven gables and the seven sins.[1] Carol Schoen[2] has shown in detail how Hawthorne carefully works out relationships between the seven gables, the seven sins, and the twenty-one chapters of the book.

Schoen sets out to prove that the first, eleventh, and twenty-first chapters reveal the effects of pride and man's limited ability to control this passion. This is the first level of the structure. The second, sixth, and tenth chapters, she claims, treat the danger of sloth; the twelfth, sixteenth, and twentieth chapters treat the sin of anger. These latter two units, which are like arches within the house, constitute the second level of structure. Within these arches are four clusters of three chapters each. Chapters 3, 4, and 5 deal with avarice (Hepzibah's attempt to run a shop); chapters 7, 8, and 9 deal with Clifford's gluttony. Chapters 13, 14, and 15 deal with the subject of lechery; and chapters 17, 18, and 19 deal with envy.

The book, according to Schoen, also contains parallel examples of how these seven sins are countered by some of the characters. She makes a detailed analysis of the action of the novel to prove her thesis.

The weakest link in her chain of evidence is in ascribing the sin of avarice to Hepzibah for attempting to run a cent-shop. Schoen claims: "Her ambition in opening the store is limited to a narrow desire for money with no apparent thought of being of service to the community through her enterprise" (Schoen, 30). She contradicts

Hawthorne's statement that Hepzibah had to earn this money or starve by pointing out that Hepzibah could have accepted help from Judge Pyncheon. Clearly, Hepzibah cannot accept such help and thus place herself even further in the power of this tyrant, let alone establish further contact with the man who condemned her brother to thirty years in jail.

Schoen is on firmer ground with her discussion of the sin of lechery. She points out that in Hawthorne's time it was impossible to discuss sexual behavior in a straightforward manner in literature. Lechery is certainly implicit in the legend of Alice Pyncheon and Matthew Maule as told by Holgrave to Phoebe. After the telling of the tale, Holgrave has established control over Phoebe through a hypnotic trance, but he renounces this power. Schoen maintains that Hawthorne believed that mesmerism was morally dangerous and possibly lewd, and he used it as a symbolic substitute for the sin of lechery. In renouncing his power over Phoebe, Holgrave triumphed over the temptation of that sin.

On the basis of her analysis, Carol Schoen claims that *The House of the Seven Gables* is "one of the most carefully structured works in American literature. Using the traditional device of the Seven Deadly Sins, Hawthorne constructed his plot, selected his incidents and probed the hidden motivations of his characters to reveal the depth of evil in the heart of man" (Schoen, 32). Her analysis is skillful and persuasive; she is undoubtedly right in her contention that a major purpose of the book is to show the effects of the seven deadly sins on human behavior. Such a scheme also fits into the allegorical pattern that Hawthorne drew from *The Pilgrim's Progress*. It is, however, not necessary to accept that Hawthorne intended such an exact correlation of each of the sins with each chapter of the book. Indeed, a strong case could be made that the subtle hypocrite Judge Jaffrey Pyncheon represents in his own person each of the seven deadly sins.

THE PARABLE OF THE RICH MAN

Calvinistic guilt and the Old Testament angry God therefore combine with Hawthorne's own melancholy sense of the past to produce dark shadows in *The House of the Seven Gables* as in all his work. Even the feasts of the book are overshadowed by death. On the very day of his greatest triumph, having thrown open his house to celebrate its completion, Colonel Pyncheon is indeed "given blood to drink," struck down with apoplexy beneath his own portrait as he sits in his study awaiting his guests. The portrait stays on in the House of the Seven Gables and casts a pall over the future until it crashes to the floor and the Pyncheons leave. "Those stern, immitigable features," Hawthorne writes, "seemed to symbolize an evil influence, and so darkly to mingle the shadow of their presence with the sunshine of the passing hour, that no good thoughts or purposes could ever spring up and blossom there. . . . [T]he ghost of a dead progenitor—perhaps as a portion of his own punishment—is often doomed to become the Evil Genius of his family" (21). The last Jaffrey Pyncheon had through his crimes and craftiness accumulated great wealth, but over him throughout the novel hangs the biblical injunction: "[I]t is easier for a camel to go through a needle's eye, than for a rich man to enter into the kingdom of God" (Luke 18: 25). The full irony of the Judge's damnation is revealed as he sits in the chair in the House of the Seven Gables. The narrator contemplates his future:

> For the Judge is a prosperous man. He cherishes his schemes, moreover, like other people, and reasonably brighter than most others; or did so, at least, as he lay abed, this morning, in an agreeable half-drowse, planning the business of the day, and speculating on the probabilities of the next fifteen years. With his firm health, and the little inroad that age has made upon him, fifteen years, or twenty— yes, or perhaps five-and-twenty!—are no more than he may fairly call his own. Five-and-twenty years for the enjoyment of his real estate in town and country, his railroad, bank, and insurance shares, his United States stock, his wealth, in short, however invested, now in possession, or soon to be acquired; together with the public hon-

ors that have fallen upon him, and the weightier ones that are yet
to fall! It is good! It is excellent! It is enough! (269–70)

This meditation is a mid–nineteenth-century version of Christ's parable of the rich man who thinks on what he will do with his wealth.
He resolves to take his ease, "eat, drink, and be merry." The parable
goes on: "But God said unto him, Thou fool, this night thy soul shall
be required of thee: then whose shall those things be, which thou hast
provided. So is he that layeth up treasure for himself, and is not rich
toward God" (Luke 12:16–21). That night, the Judge's soul is required
of him; and the things he has acquired go to the rejected ones, Clifford
and Hepzibah.

All the power, wealth, and knowledge of the Pyncheon family is
thus ineffectual. The Biblical warrant for this theme is found in Jeremiah: "Thus saith the Lord. Let not the wise man glory in his wisdom,
neither let the mighty man glory in his might, let not the rich man
glory in his riches" (Jer. 9: 23). And again in Zechariah: "Not by
might, nor by power, but by my spirit, saith the Lord of hosts" (Zech.
4: 6).

The Judge is one of "the scribes and Pharisees, hypocrites," that
Christ describes as "whited sepulchres, which indeed appear beautiful
outward, but are within full of dead men's bones, and of all unclean-
ness" (Matt. 23: 27). Hawthorne is careful to emphasize the beautiful
outward appearance of the Judge: his "white neckcloth of almost
snowy purity," the polish of his boots, his gold-headed cane, and so
on, but all this conceals the blackness of his corruption. He is "out-
wardly righteous unto men, but within . . . full of hypocrisy and iniquity" (Matt. 23: 28). The most powerful metaphor of this inner
corruption is in Hawthorne's image of the "tall and stately edifice,"
which in the opinion of the rich man and of others is "the man's character, or the man himself" (229). This metaphoric building is a nineteenth-century version of the House of the Seven Gables, so splendidly
built by the first Pyncheon. Hawthorne writes, "Behold, therefore, a
palace! Its splendid halls and suites of spacious apartments are floored
with a mosaic-work of costly marbles; its windows, the whole height

of each room, admit the sunshine through the most transparent of plate-glass; its high cornices are gilded, and its ceilings gorgeously painted; and a lofty dome—through which, from the central pavement, you may gaze up to the sky, as with no obstructing medium between—surmounts the whole" (229). But beneath the marble pavement, "in a stagnant water-puddle," or in some closet, "may lie a corpse, half-decayed, and still decaying, and diffusing its death-scent all through the palace!" (230). The images of space, light, and rich color are all delusive: they constitute merely the whited sepulchre for the corpse—the dead soul—within.

CLIFFORD AS CHRIST FIGURE

The strength of spirit is found ultimately in a weak vessel, Clifford. Strange as it may seem, Hawthorne portrays the ineffectual Clifford in various subtle ways as a type of Christ. Clifford pays for the sins of the Pyncheons with his suffering of thirty years (the lifetime of Christ) in jail. Christ, according to Philippians, was made by God in the likeness of men, and "made himself of no reputation, and took upon him the form of a servant" (Phil. 2: 7). In this role as suffering servant, like Clifford, Christ was "despised and rejected" (Isa. 53: 3). Even Clifford's pathetic childishness is reminiscent of Christ's injunction, "Verily I say unto you, Except ye be converted, and become as little children, ye shall not enter into the kingdom of heaven" (Matt. 18: 3). In the weakness and helplessness of Clifford we see an embodiment of Christ's advice to his disciples: "Take my yoke upon you, and learn of me; for I am meek and lowly in heart: and ye shall find rest unto your souls" (Matt. 11: 29). In Clifford's weakness and foolishness there is the repeated message of the New Testament, that such is the Kingdom of Heaven. As Paul said, "But God has chosen the foolish things of the world to confound the wise; and God hath chosen the weak things of the world to confound the things which are mighty" (1 Cor. 1: 27). In addition, like Christ, Clifford is referred to as a second Adam (150). His face is a "record of infinite sorrow," which recalls Christ who is described in Isaiah as "a man of sorrows" (Isa. 53: 31). There is also a reference to Christ's crown of thorns at his crucifixion in Clifford's desire to be pricked by a rose thorn (150).

Clifford's sacrificial role is central to the meaning of the novel. Through him, the house of Pyncheon is cleansed and redeemed from the repeated cycle of death and damnation. To support this theme, the novel has several references to birds and the cleansing of the house. The source for this ritual is Leviticus, in which the instructions for cleansing and purifying a house are laid down. The priest has to take two birds and "shall kill the one of the birds in an earthen vessel over running water"; the other bird is dipped in the blood of the dead one and into running water and then used to sprinkle the house seven times (Lev. 14: 49–52). Clifford and Hepzibah are often referred to as two birds; Clifford has associations with the dead bird, and Hepzibah with the living. Clifford is associated with the smell of earth and with clods; Hepzibah is seen as one who is ministering to the restoration to life. Clifford "had a singular propensity . . . to hang over Maule's Well" (153), which is analogous to the bird killed over the running water as the ritual cleansing of the house. This is the well, it will be remembered, whose pure waters turned foul after the first Pyncheon built his house over the site of Maule's cottage. This well in the end throws up a succession of kaleidoscopic pictures of the coming good fortunes of the family after they leave the house. In these ceremonies of cleansing and renewal, however, it is important to note the role played also by the burgeoning love of Holgrave and Phoebe, who "transfigured the earth, and made it Eden again" (307).[3]

GOOD AND EVIL

The biblical emphasis on light and darkness as the equivalents of good and evil prevails throughout the novel. Phoebe is always surrounded by light and freshness. Her presence banishes the shadows of the old house. Holgrave, too, is associated with light through his occupation as a daguerreotypist. Judge Pyncheon, on the other hand, is associated with darkness. He has "a dark, full-fed physiognomy" (118). When attempting to see Clifford in the House of the Seven Gables, he puts aside Phoebe with "a voice as deep as a thunder-growl, and with a frown as black as the cloud whence it issues" (126). The blackness of his threat and presence darkens Clifford's life until the Judge dies and the shadow is at last lifted.

Throughout the novel, the Judge is identified with Satan, also known as Apollyon in *The Pilgrim's Progress*. The Judge always looks and tries to behave like a gentleman—the devil's traditional guise—but his inner nature is always betraying him. When he is thwarted in his attempt to kiss Phoebe, she considers him as hard as a rock and as cold as the east wind. He attempts to mask his frustration, however, with the "dog-day heat" of his apparent benevolence, but appears to her instead "very much like a serpent, which, as a preliminary to fascination, is said to fill the air with his peculiar odor" (119). The reference to the serpent tempting Eve in the Garden is clear enough, but this Eve is proof against his wiles. When, soon after, the Judge is thwarted in his attempts to force an entrance into the House of the Seven Gables to see Clifford, "a red fire kindled in his eyes," an indication of his "hot fellness of purpose." This expression, the Author comments, comes "darkening forth . . . out of the whole man" (129).

Hawthorne is, however, far too subtle a moralist to give all the devilment to the Judge. Satan's handiwork is visible also even in the childhood cunning of the gingerbread cake consumer, Ned Higgins, as well as in his unbridled passion of wrath when he finds the cent-shop closed after Hepzibah and Clifford have fled. Even in the organ-grinder's monkey there is visible what the Author calls "the deviltry of nature" (164) and the image of Mammon, the least of Milton's fallen angels. The demonic impulse is visible in the Maule inheritance too. The first Maule was a reputed wizard, and "the family eye," says the Author, is said by the townsfolk "to possess strange power" (26). Matthew Maule is given demonic powers in Holgrave's tale, which Holgrave also apparently possesses and is tempted to use over Phoebe. Yet he renounces these powers out of his reverence for her integrity, and in so doing breaks the long chain of evil.

The Bible

After Judge Pyncheon's death, which ends his evil influence on the House of the Seven Gables, the house is washed clean by a storm. At the end, the sunshine and "the wide benediction of the sky" look down on the house. Alice's posies are in full bloom, "a mystic expression that something within the house was consummated" (284–86). The "long and black calamity" (112) that had been Clifford's life has been lightened at last, and his suffering proves redemptive for the whole Pyncheon family. Thus the pattern of Original Sin and consequent punishment characteristic of so many of the books of the Old Testament is finally broken by the promise of redemption found in the New. The whole texture of *The House of the Seven Gables* is deepened and enriched by these repeated allusions to biblical text.

Yet, even when all the characters leave the house at the end of the novel to go to live in the country, amid the joy of release and departure there is a tinge of melancholy for what is being lost, ironically felt most of all by Holgrave. Settling down means the end of his youth and high idealism. In a pregnant passage earlier in the book, Hawthorne had commented: "What is there so ponderous in evil, that a thumb's bigness of it should outweigh the mass of things not evil, which were heaped into the other scale!" (231). In "The Fall of the House of Usher" Poe had the house crumble into the tarn as the guilty brother and sister perish. But there is no cataclysmic destruction of the House of the Seven Gables, which still stands at the end of the novel, guarding, it seems, "the image of awful Death" (305) that pervaded it when the body of the Judge was seated in the chair in the parlor. In the happiest of his novelistic endings, Hawthorne cannot let go of his propensity for "the blackness of darkness" that Herman Melville saw as the ultimate expression of his art.

10

The Narrative:
Intention and Design

THE PREFACE

Hawthorne's intention in writing *The House of the Seven Gables* is clearly laid out in his preface, which is worth examining at length, for it tells us, at least in part, what we can legitimately expect of this fiction. He begins by claiming for himself the traditional latitude allowed the author of a romance. The novel, he notes, aims at minute fidelity and conforms "to the probable and ordinary course of man's experience" (1). The romancer, however, has the right to present "the truth of the human heart" under circumstances of the author's own choosing. Hawthorne claims for himself the freedom of a painter—and he was no doubt thinking of the so-called picturesque movement—"to bring out or mellow the lights and deepen and enrich the shadows of the picture" (1).

The privilege of the romancer also enables him to mingle what he calls "the Marvelous" with the actual substance of the tale. The essence of the romantic in this book is, for Hawthorne, connecting a bygone time with the present—that is to say, making history live into the contemporaneous world by means of legend. One definition of legend is "an unauthenticated story from earlier times, preserved by tradition and popularly thought to be historical." This, I think, is the meaning that Hawthorne intends, rather than the more currently popular meaning of legend as a tale that is essentially unreal or untrue. Again, Hawthorne evokes "the picturesque effect" in his use of legend as a way of shading with gray "the broad daylight" of the present.

Hawthorne goes on to note that many writers lay stress on "some definite moral purpose" in their work, and he intends not to be deficient in this respect. Again, the tone is slightly ironic, but the moral that Hawthorne claims for the book is certainly one that haunts many of his notebook entries: "that the wrong-doing of one generation lives into the successive ones, and, divesting itself of every temporary advantage, becomes a pure and uncontrollable mischief" (2). He added that he would feel gratified if he could convince even one man of the folly of passing on riches onto the heads of unfortunate posterity, but adds, wistfully, if not cynically, that he has not the slightest hope of success in this endeavor.

When romance teaches anything, he goes on, it is usually through a far more subtle process than the ostensible one. What was Hawthorne's subtle moral intention? The question has intrigued many critics; and there is no consensus on the answer. Here again *The Pilgrim's Progress* may be the best guide. Clifford and Hepzibah make the redemptive pilgrimage away from Giant Despair, while Phoebe acts like Hopeful in leading Holgrave away from Despair to the Celestial City of marital bliss. The ending of generations of wrongdoing is dependent on redemptive suffering and the rediscovery of hope.

Hawthorne ends his preface with the customary disclaimer of the fictionist: that the location of the story is imaginary and that the characters of the romance are of his own making, or "of his own mixing." Such freedom from specifics, he thought, was necessary in order to avoid the possibility of dangerous criticism resulting from bringing his "fancy-pictures almost into positive contact with the realities of the moment" (3).

The connections between *Seven Gables* and Salem, however, were unmistakable from the first. Unfortunately, Hawthorne named his chief characters the Pyncheons, after a local family. Quite understandably, they vigorously objected to being subjected to the derision and contempt consequent on this fictional treatment. Hawthorne told his publisher J. T. Fields soon after the book was published that a man called Peter Oliver had written to tell him that there had been a Judge Pynchon, his grandfather, living in Salem at the time of the American Revolution who was also a Tory. Hawthorne continued, "There are several touches, in my account of the Pyncheons, which, he says, makes it probable that I had this actual family in my eye, and he considers himself infinitely wronged and aggrieved, and thinks it monstrous that the 'virtuous dead' cannot be suffered to rest quietly in their graves." Another Pynchon, a clergyman, who lived near Hawthorne, was also highly indignant. "Who would have dreamed," Hawthorne wrote, "of claimants starting up, for such an inheritance as the House of the Seven Gables!" (*Letters*, 16: 435–36).

These claimants cost Hawthorne a good deal of time and trouble. They demanded apologies and tried to get him to change the name in the book's subsequent editions. As Hawthorne explained to the Reverend Pynchon, he got the name out of old records and believed that the original Pyncheon had returned to England and left no descendants. He thought that it was inconceivable that any reader could think that he was writing "a genuine family history, under the genuine family name," since it treated matters of "the most intimate privacy" and ended with the death of its most noted member in the present day. All that Hawthorne could promise this Pynchon and all the others was that future editions would carry his guarantee that he intended no resemblance of his characters to anyone living or dead (*Letters*, 16: 445–47). The Pynchon family apparently had to be content with this guarantee. In another letter to Fields Hawthorne estimated that there were about twenty "Pyncheon jackasses" extant and wondered how long he would be bothered by them. He ironically suggested to Fields that he publish the whole correspondence and anticipated a great run for the volume (*Letters*, 16: 443).

Hawthorne was being a bit disingenuous when he denied all allegations that the book had any relation with the real Salem. His plea that the book be read strictly as a romance that had "more to do with the clouds overhead, than with any portion of the actual soil of the County of Essex" (3) has always been ignored. Local history and Hawthorne's family history have been sources for a good deal of the critical controversy that the book has always generated. Hawthorne wanted both to have his cake and eat it: to deal with an actual historical place and real characters, and at the same time claim the latitude of the fairy tale maker.

NARRATIVE METHOD

The narrative method of *The House of the Seven Gables* is quite complex, a blending of realistic and romantic conventions that often gives Hawthorne trouble. In the preface Hawthorne sets up a dialogue between a narrator in the third person, called Author, and his imagined audience, called Reader—a dialogue that is continued, from time to time, throughout the rest of the book. This form of address is based on an eighteenth-century novelistic convention in which the author freely enters his own narrative and addresses the reader. Fielding frequently uses this device in his novels, but he invariably uses the first person, as in *Tom Jones* where the "I" assumes the jovial guise of an hospitable innkeeper. Hawthorne uses the first-person singular, like Fielding, in the first paragraph of the novel. After that he occasionally uses the editorial first-person plural, "we." For the most part, however, he is the invisible third-person Author, ever present in the narrative, but self-effacing.

The Character of the Author By using the third person in this manner, Hawthorne both enters and distances himself from his narrative. For the most part this third-person narrator is invisible, and all but omniscient, a God who enters the minds of his characters and knows not only all about them but also about their family and local history. This Author, or what has come recently to be called the implied author, is by no means the jovial host as in *Tom Jones*, but is rather a cautious, whimsical, sometimes sentimental and coy, and often moralistic man who feels free to intrude at any time into his narrative.

This implied Author is not to be identified with Hawthorne, who was, I believe, much less sentimental and moralistic than the so-called and self-styled Author of *Seven Gables*. Moreover, there are self-imposed limitations to this Author's omniscience. This is evident in his frequent refusal to attribute exclusive causes for events. The Author uses what Yvor Winters has called "the formula of alternate possibilities."[1] That is to say, he provides two sets of explanations for some events, a natural and a supernatural.

The Author begins the narrative with a historical account of how Colonel Pyncheon acquired the land of Matthew Maule through the condemnation and death of Maule on the charge of witchcraft. Then he tells of the building of the house, the feast that celebrated its opening, and the finding of the dead body of the Colonel seated under his picture. The doctor rules that the cause of death was apoplexy, but the narrator points out that there are rumors of murder and also a tradition that the curse had caused the death, as well as the tainting of Maule's Well.

As the novel unfolds, three other Pyncheons die under similarly mysterious circumstances; and in each case the cause could be natural or supernatural in origin. An inherited tendency towards apoplexy and perhaps a guilty conscience could cause the deaths; the operation of the curse could also be the agent. The Author shrouds the issues with "supposes," "maybes," "perhapses," "possiblys," and "it is saids." Similarly, the slow decline of the Pyncheon family can be ascribed to aristocratic pretension and genetic failure possibly through incestuous mating or to the curse and the consequent loss of the title to the eastern lands. The first explanation belongs to the daylight world of reason and realism; the second belongs to the twilight world of imagination and romance. Hawthorne attempts to balance the novel equally between the two.

The coy and sentimental side of the narrator—an irritating convention at best—appears early in the novel, at the end of the first

The Narrative

chapter, after Hawthorne's description of the house. "And now" the narrator says, "in a very humble way, as will be seen—we proceed to open our narrative" (29). This coy note is continued in the chapter that immediately follows, wherein Hepzibah is seen getting out of bed. "Far from us be the indecorum of assisting," the narrator writes, "even in imagination, at a maiden lady's toilet!" Hepzibah finishes her prayers, but instead of beginning the story the narrator asks: "Will she now issue forth over the threshold of our story?" (30–31). No: the narrator watches her fidget about with a miniature painting of her brother and then with a mirror. At last we find out why the narrator is so reluctant to begin: "All this time, however, we are loitering faint-heartedly on the threshold of our story" (34). Why? Because the narrator is reluctant to talk about this decayed aristocrat setting up a cent-shop.

All this fooling around is in effect an elaborate way of mocking poor Hepzibah's pretensions, which he does for the rest of the chapter. At the end of it he confesses: "that so much of the mean and ludicrous should be hopelessly mixed up with the purest pathos" (40–41) is "a heavy annoyance" for a writer who tries to represent nature. It has to be admitted that the tone the author adopts is pretty annoying for the reader too. Hawthorne seems to be implying that finding the right tone for representing Hepzibah has been difficult for him. In fact, tone seems to trouble him for the first half of the novel, both in terms of characterization and setting. In chapter 10, for example, in describing the details of the Pyncheon garden, the narrator confesses again to the reader, "The author needs great faith in his reader's sympathy; else he must hesitate to give details so minute, and incidents apparently so trifling, as are essential to make up the idea of this garden-life" (150).

This story of inherited curses, and evil spreading down through the generations, is also intended as a comedy. Also Hawthorne is always striving to strike a convincing balance between realism and romance. So even when the narrator discusses the most ordinary and everyday matters, such as the opening of Hepzibah's cent-shop and the arrival of Phoebe, he has to be careful to introduce matters of romance, whether it be Hepzibah's fantasy about the arrival of a rich relation from India, or speculation about the "natural magic" or "homely witchcraft" of Phoebe's housekeeping abilities. The arrival of Clifford at the house after thirty years in jail is surrounded by a ghostly air. When they first meet in the cent-shop, Phoebe sees the solidly real Judge Pyncheon as the ghost of his Puritan ancestor. On the other hand, Old Uncle Venner is intended to be a homespun, realistic character with a contemplative turn of mind who brings a down-to-earth, commonsense philosophy to the interpretation of events.

As Author, Hawthorne also reserves for himself the privilege of psychological or philosophic summary. After the end of the chapter describing the Sunday afternoon tea party in "The Pyncheon Garden," the Author steps in and comments on the ruin of Clifford's body and mind and adds that his happiness in the garden is illusory. The illusory happiness then becomes a kind of metaphor for the novel itself: "Why not? If not the thing itself, it is marvelously like it, and the more so for that ethereal and intangible quality, which causes it all to vanish, at too close an introspection. Take it, therefore, while you may. Murmur not—question not—but make the most of it!" (158).

The Author plays throughout with the ironies of illusion: the existence of happiness in the midst of misery and the presence of life and music in the midst of death. The Italian organ-grinder, for example, plays away outside the House of the Seven Gables while the body of the Judge reposes within. The Author comments ironically that it would be an ugly business if the Judge, "who would not have cared a fig for Paganini's fiddle, in his most harmonious mood" (294–95), should appear at the door in his blood-stained shirt-bosom and drive this "foreign vagabond away" (295). The grinding out of waltzes and jigs goes on while within there is only the silence of death. The Author adds: "This contrast, or intermingling of tragedy with mirth, happens daily, hourly, momently" (295). Hawthorne tries to show that the borderline between tragedy and comedy, between song and solemn symphony, between appearance and reality, between realism and romance, between life and fiction, is in the end most difficult, if not impossible, to distinguish.

Indeed, Clifford lives in a world that is part dream and part waking. This is shown most effectively and sensitively in chapter 11, "The Arched Window." Sometimes he feels he would like to break out of his somnambulistic state and into the world of reality. He is tempted to throw himself out of the arched window into the life of the street below. On another occasion, he and Hepzibah try to join the worshipers in church. But these attempts fail: the hold of the past is too strong and the fear of the present too great. Clifford falls back again into the safety of his dream life. The most effective symbol of this process is when he is blowing bubbles from the window, which drift down "in hues bright as imagination" to the street below. He finds delight in this occupation until a bubble floats down and breaks against the nose of Judge Pyncheon who happens to be passing. "What! Still blowing soap-bubbles!" the Judge cries contemptuously (171–72). This touch of reality destroys not only the bubble but also Clifford's precarious contentment; he collapses in a palsy of fear. This scene is a foreshadowing of the fatal incursion of the Judge into the House of the Seven Gables. When that happens, however, and the Judge dies as a consequence, there is an ironic reversal of the bubble image. Commenting on the death, the Author notes, "At his decease, there is only a vacancy, and a momentary eddy—very small, as compared with the apparent magnitude of the ingurgitated object—and a bubble or two, ascending out of the black depth, and bursting at the surface" (309). For all his power and wealth, the Judge's death makes a bubble no more substantial than those of Clifford. As Darrel Abel has observed, "The question between Clifford and the Judge (as between Hawthorne and the world which appear to undervalue his bright imaginations) was: Whose bubbles are finally more real, the 'airy spheres' of the artist or the 'solid unrealities' of the Judge, whose life ends like a bubble."[2]

Holgrave Narrates In the midpoint of the novel, Hawthorne hands over the narrative completely to one of the characters, Holgrave. The daguerreotypist tells Phoebe the story of Alice Pyncheon and her enslavement by the carpenter, Matthew Maule—a story within a story. This "legend," as Holgrave calls it, is interesting not only for formal reasons, but also for what it tells us about earlier versions of the narrative. We learn that Matthew Maule has inherited necromantic powers from his grandfather, the original Maule, which he exerts over Alice. According to Holgrave, then, there was some justification in Maule's condemnation as a witch. Moreover, the original Matthew Maule has retained his powers beyond death and has "as little hesitation or difficulty in rising out of his grave, as an ordinary man in getting out of bed" (189); he particularly likes to haunt the House of the Seven Gables.

Gervase Pyncheon's object in inviting Matthew Maule to his house is to persuade him to reveal the secret of the hidden deeds to the eastern lands. It turns out that Maule is willing to help in this endeavor on two conditions: first, that if Maule is successful in finding the deeds, Pyncheon will make over the House of the Seven Gables to Maule, and second, that Pyncheon will allow Maule to use his daughter as an instrument in the search for the deeds. In the Faustian bargain that Pyncheon strikes, greed overcomes natural feelings. In the crucial moment when Alice faintly calls for help from the wizard's spell, her father ignores her. He repeats his grandfather's crime of abusing and destroying another for his own financial gain. As Gordon Hutner suggests, the father is even willing to betray his daughter and sell her into sexual bondage with his sworn enemy to gain his ends.[3] But, so great is the power of the curse, that Maule is unable to persuade the spirits of his ancestors, through the medium of Alice, to reveal the hiding place. "The custody of this secret," he tells Pyncheon, "that would so enrich his heirs, makes part of your grandfather's retribution. He must choke with it, until it is no longer of any value. And keep you the House of the Seven Gables! It is too dear bought an inheritance, and too heavy, with the curse upon it, to be shifted yet awhile from the Colonel's posterity!" (207).

But, quite unjustly, having failed to gain the secret, Maule does not then release Alice from the spell. She remains his slave until her death, which is caused by Maule's willfulness. Holgrave's story tells us a good deal about the romantic, twilight aspect of the novel. First, the curse is mutual: the Faustian pact binds both Pyncheons and Maules through a chain of years until the time is finally ripe for breaking it. Lineage or inheritance, whether for good or evil, is a powerful force that the mere will of the inheritors cannot break. The force seems to work on a historical, as well as a personal level. The aristocratic, colonial heritage, presented attractively in this story as in earlier ones, in images of art works, fine furniture, and rich, brocaded clothes, survives through the generations.

The narrative method permits Hawthorne to take advantage of both romance and realism. Holgrave is telling the tale as a historical romance and is therefore allowed all the trappings of the genre, unfettered by alternative, realistic possibilities. But the reader is, of course, expected to take this into account in assessing the value and truth of the tale by the standards of realism. The Author takes care to embellish the setting in which the tale has been told. The moon is rising over the garden of the old house; its commonplace characteristics, "which, at noontide," the narrator comments, "it seemed to have taken a century of sordid life to accumulate—were now transfigured by a charm of romance" (213).

Phoebe, too, has learned from the tale, as she has from her experience of looking after the aging Pyncheons in the House of the Seven Gables. "I never cared much about moonlight before," she says. "It seems as if I had looked at everything hitherto, in broad daylight, or else in the ruddy light of a cheerful fire, glimmering and dancing through a room" (214). Like Holgrave, she has learned that the common light of day is not sufficient to illuminate all of life's mysteries, and is moving away from her heedless youth towards what Holgrave calls "a youth regained" (215), one based on awareness, not ignorance. She is also moving, unconsciously, toward love for Holgrave as he moves toward her, so that they meet in that "neutral territory," as Hawthorne calls it, between romance and realism. For them, the old garden, with its age-old soil of evil has become "virgin soil," a "bower in Eden, blossoming with the earliest roses God ever made" (214).

The Return of the Author Hawthorne resumes his role as Author in the following chapter, "Phoebe's Good Bye," in which she leaves the house on "the wings of the morning" (222) for a short visit to her home. In the absence of this guardian angel, the demonic Judge gains entry into the House of the Seven Gables and precipitates the climax of the novel.

For this event the Author resorts to a standard device of the Gothic romance: the pathetic fallacy. This device matches the weather to the events of the fiction. Phoebe's sun gives way to an easterly storm that sinks Clifford and Hepzibah into a depression. The Judge seeks entry into the house to see Clifford, weeping crocodile tears in what Hepzibah calls a "loathesome pretence of affection for your victim!" (228). His object is the same as that of Gervase in Holgrave's legend, "Alice's Posies": he believes that Clifford knows where the clues to the undiscovered wealth of old Jaffrey Pyncheon are hidden and he is determined to force the knowledge out of Clifford.

The Author uses the chapter "The Scowl and the Smile" to moralize on the nature of hypocrisy and to start the attack on the Judge that is continued so relentlessly in "Governor Pyncheon." The scowl belongs to the hapless Hepzibah and it conceals her timidity and loving heart. The smile belongs to the Judge and it in turn conceals his ruthless audacity and grasping selfishness. In this moral lecture, the Author makes use once more of the metaphor of the house for the human heart. The Judge builds a magnificent mansion of pretense to conceal the pool of stagnant water tinged with blood that is the reality of his character. The Author uses a number of striking oxymorons to illustrate the hypocritical nature of the man, such as "solid unrealities" and "splendid rubbish." The Judge is firmly convinced of the reality of wealth and property—in fact he is convinced that they are the only realities. When Hepzibah points out that he has more than enough wealth for his remaining years, and that in persecuting Clifford he is merely continuing the inherited family curse, his reply is simply: "Talk sense, Hepzibah, for Heaven's sake!" (237). Yet, this is probably the most sensible advice he has ever received. He tells Hepzibah that he will have Clifford placed in the madhouse if she does not do his bidding and fetch him. He sinks down into the fatal Pyncheon chair to await Clifford's arrival; and the Author is careful to point out that he is not only sad and weary, but also exercising a great effort of will to remain calm. His brow assumes a "black-purple" hue as he waits.

Hepzibah's View The next chapter, "Clifford's Chamber," is told from Hepzibah's point of view, because Hawthorne wants to make the movements of the other characters unknown and mysterious. Slowly and painfully, with many delays, she goes to find her brother, but discovers that he is not in his room nor apparently anywhere else in the house. The Author, however, makes the occasional observation on her thoughts, and the limits of her thoughts. Commenting on the depths of her despair, he adds: "But Hepzibah did not see, that, just as there comes a warm sunbeam into every cottage-window, so comes a love-beam of God's care and pity, for every separate need" (245). This kind of sentiment is the stuff of nineteenth-century women's fiction and a return to the coy, pietistic tone of the earlier part of the novel. The employment of this tone seems, once again, to be part of Hawthorne's conscious effort to brighten up the work. There are, certainly, few sunbeams in the rest of this chapter as Hepzibah's unsuccessful search for her brother causes her to speculate on the possibility that he has escaped from the house. If he has done so, she thinks, he may already have incurred public disgrace because of his crazy behavior in the streets, or he may have committed suicide. Finally, however, having been forced to the extreme measure of running back to the Judge to seek his help, she discovers her brother on the very threshold of the room where the Judge lies dead. Clifford, imitating Christian in *The Pilgrim's Progress*, tells Hepzibah that they must escape from this dungeon of Giant Despair before the corpse starts up and catches them.

Authorial Variations The following chapter, "The Flight of the Two Owls," unlike the others, is told almost entirely in the form of dramatic dialogue, with a small amount of editorial comment from the Author at the beginning. This method serves to objectify the state of mind of brother and sister and to increase suddenly the pace of the narrative. The escape from the house works for Clifford but not for Hepzibah, who psychologically cannot leave the house, even when the pair of them are flying through the countryside on the train. For Clifford, on the other hand, so great is his sense of escape from the dungeon and so excited is he by his rate of travel that he proposes to the old man on the train that permanent houses be abolished altogether. The journey, however, is soon over; Clifford's exhilaration is less durable than Hepzibah's despair. The House of the Seven Gables reexerts its baleful influence and the two owls abjectly return to their dark roost.

After this fine chapter, Hawthorne loses control of his narrative again in chapter 18, which contains one of the most curious episodes in the history of fiction. In "Governor Pyncheon" the Author, in an absurdly jocular tone, addresses, questions, lectures, and abuses the corpse of the Judge. The omniscient Author is fully apprised of all the Judge's many appointments of that fatal day and tells of each one with a gloating satisfaction in all the glorious opportunities for money and power missed. The Judge, of course, is quite unable to defend himself. This chapter is a kangaroo court with a vengeance. It has been plausibly surmised that the chapter was Hawthorne's revenge on the politician who fired him from his post in the Customhouse, a man who bore several similarities to the Judge. This could account for the personal savagery with which this chapter is endowed, a savagery that also makes the Judge a powerful symbol of all the world's hypocrites.

Not content with addressing himself to one generation, the Author then summons the ghosts of all the dead Pyncheons from the first Puritan colonel down to the latest, the son of Judge Pyncheon, who has recently died in Europe, and the ghost of the Judge himself: "We are tempted," he writes as Author, "to make a little sport with the idea [of all the Pyncheons coming out of their graves]" (279). He gives in to temptation and overdoes it badly. All the ghosts advance to the picture of the Colonel and try to move it to see behind it. Each fails. All this mockery and heavy irony become wearisome. Hawthorne himself is conscious of his offenses: "Indulging our fancy in this freak" he confesses, "we have partly lost the power of restraint and guidance" (280).

Having apologized for this strange diversion, the Author returns to the corpse as a new day dawns. A mouse and then a fly, emblems of decay, invade the body. The Author asks whether the Judge will rise to resume his business or to repent. But it is too late. There is no repentance and there will be no return to the land of the living.

The "Governor Pyncheon" chapter shows effectively enough how man's physical and political power and ambitions are the shadows of shadows, the dreams of dreams. The solid realities are decay and inevitable death. Behind those realities is Original Sin, brought into the world through Adam's disobedience in eating the forbidden fruit of the tree of knowledge, from which stems man's pride and delusion of self-sufficiency. Great plans, houses, gold, overweening ambition, and hope for the future all dissolve into delusion and shadow in the face of the death of the body and, more seriously, the death of the soul. Hawthorne in chapter 18 is relentlessly drawing the moral of the biblical injunction: "For what shall it profit a man, if he shall gain the whole world, and lose his own soul?" (Mark 8: 36). The Author then takes leave of the body of Judge Pyncheon and takes the reader into the light of day at the front of the House of the Seven Gables for the next chapter.

In the next two chapters Hawthorne is again in full control of his work. From the uneasy exercise in fantasy, with the corpse of the Judge, the Author returns to reality with Uncle Venner, always the touchstone in the novel. He is the first person to appear in this chapter, "Alice's Posies." The storm has blown over and the sun is shining, so it is time for Phoebe to return. But before she returns, the Author gives the reader two important symbols as a sign that the book is moving toward a happy resolution. First, one of the branches of the Pyncheon elm has turned to bright gold. "It was like a golden branch," he writes, "that gained Aeneas and the Sibyl admittance into Hades" (285).

This reference points the reader to a crucial scene in *The Aeneid* in which Aeneas, accompanied by a prophetess, is admitted into the underworld with the golden bough as his safe passport to the realms of the dead. Here he meets the former rulers who are the progenitors of the great city of Rome that Aenaeas will found.

The Author does not say outright who is the Aeneas of his story, but it becomes obvious later that Holgrave is the first person to enter the house after Clifford and Hepzibah have left. Before that time any number of people try to gain entry but fail. Uncle Venner, Ned Higgins, tradesmen, and passersby eddy around the house in a current of life and activity that mocks the dead body within. After Holgrave, Phoebe arrives back from her mother's house, now "graver, more womanly" (297), as the Author comments. She is warned by Ned Higgins, the gingerbread eater, not to go in, but she is swiftly drawn into the house by someone invisible—another touch of the Gothic romance.

In the next chapter, "The Flower of Eden," the mysterious person is revealed as Holgrave. The golden bough gives him and Phoebe immunity to death as it did for Aeneas and the Sibyl. When Holgrave reveals that the Judge is dead, this knowledge in the face of the world's ignorance binds the couple mysteriously together. "The image of awful Death," the Author comments, "which filled the house, held them united by his stiffened grasp" (305). This grim psychological insight is typical of Hawthorne at his best. The image of the Judge's body had struck the dreamer and reformer Holgrave hard: it made him see the reality of guilt and retribution and made him see, also, the evanescence of life.

When Holgrave admits Phoebe into the house it is not only to reveal the death of the Judge, but also to ask for her help. He is no self-reliant hero, like Aeneas, but a dependent and unnerved man who has been cowed by the sight of the Judge's corpse. She tells him that they must reveal the death to the world; but before he follows her advice and throws open the doors of the house, he revels in their shared secret of the death of the Judge: "It separated Phoebe and himself from the world, and bound them to each other, by their exclusive knowledge" (305). This secret knowledge awakens sentiments of love that would otherwise have taken longer to blossom, or given their shared New England reticence, may not have even developed at all. "I never hoped to feel young again!" he tells Phoebe, "The world looked strange, wild, evil, hostile;—my past life, so lonesome and dreary; my future, a shapeless gloom" (306). He confesses his dependence on

Phoebe and his love for her. She in turn confesses her love for him. Their love has an immediately transfiguring effect on each. As the Author expresses it rhetorically, sentimentally, and romantically, "The bliss, which makes all things true, beautiful, and holy, shone around this youth and maiden. They were conscious of nothing sad nor old. They transfigured the earth, and made it Eden again, and themselves the two first dwellers in it. The dead man, so close beside them, was forgotten. At such a crisis, there is no Death; for Immortality is revealed anew, and embraces everything in its hallowed atmosphere" (307).

Their knowledge of the Judge's death has, paradoxically, enabled them to find love. The secret first binds them together in a kind of complicity of sin, but their decision to reveal the secret to the world enables them to declare their love. Beneath Hawthorne's sentiment lies his tragic sense that death and life are closely commingled, and, since the Fall of Man and the loss of paradise the knowledge of death and evil makes human sexual love possible. Through such love, and within its limitations, paradise can be regained. According to the doctrine of *felix culpa*, the fortunate fall, there can be no true goodness or innocence in the ignorance of evil.

Fortune smiles again upon Holgrave and Phoebe, for just as they are about to announce the death, and thus inevitably throw suspicion on the absent Clifford and Hepzibah, that couple returns from their railway journey to confront the dead body and find themselves not alone. Clifford realizes what has happened between Holgrave and Phoebe. Alice's posies have bloomed again—an emblem of her released spirit: "And so," he adds, "the flower of Eden has bloomed, likewise, in this old, darksome house, to-day!" (308). Another symbolic object, Alice's posies, also protects Phoebe. Now in full bloom from the seeds brought from Italy by Alice long ago, the flowers seem, according to the Author, "a mystic expression that something within the house was consummated" (286). The curse has finally been lifted by the death of the Judge. The curse will not be continued by further vengeance because the cycle has been broken by the union of Phoebe and Holgrave. "I have heard," Holgrave tells Uncle Venner, in a comment that has sexual and allegorical overtones, "that the water of Maule's Well suits [Alice's posies] best" (288).

As in the last act of a Shakespearean comedy, the last chapter, "The Departure," ties up all the loose ends and distributes rewards and prizes. Many readers have felt that it is all too neat and tidy; it follows the formula not only of romantic comedy but also of detective fiction in which all the strange clues are gathered up and put into a neat pattern that explains all the mysteries. Holgrave plays the role of the sleuth in this chapter. His methods are, however, somewhat unorthodox. Hawthorne uses his familiar doctrine of alternate possibilities to report that "many persons affirmed" (311) that Holgrave used a mesmerist to gain the information that cleared the name of Clifford and laid the blame for old Jaffrey Pyncheon's death where it belonged, on the Judge. This knowledge is followed by the equally felicitous information from overseas, confirming the ghostly appearance in the "Governor Pyncheon" chapter, that the Judge's son has died.

The deaths of the Judge and his heir clear the way for the inheritance to pass to Hepzibah, Clifford, and Phoebe, and thus, through her, to Holgrave. There is another legacy of the death too: "a permanently invigorating and ultimately beneficial effect on Clifford" (313). It is as if some of the Judge's energy and will have been passed on to his cousin, as well as his wealth.

The last mystery is solved when Holgrave touches the secret spring that causes the picture of the Colonel to move aside and reveal the long-hidden titles to the eastern lands; the picture then falls to the ground because the machinery that has held it in place has rusted through. The dynastic hold on the house is thus broken. The secret has been passed down through the Maule family; and it is now revealed that the secret was discovered by Clifford when he was a child. The Judge's memory of this discovery, which prompted him to want to question Clifford, was then correct. But there are no other documents hidden behind the picture as the Judge had hoped, so the discovery is now worthless, because the titles to the eastern lands have long since been superseded by other claims and by settlement. The hard realist Jaffrey Pyncheon had been pursuing a worthless dream all along.

The Narrative

The time has come to leave the House of the Seven Gables. The Author in his final editorial comments on the story does not sentimentalize Clifford's and Hepzibah's farewell to the house, which they quit "with hardly more emotion than if they had made it their arrangement to return thither at tea-time" (318). Ancestral and incestuous ties are thus quickly broken. Uncle Venner, also included among the new household arrangements at the Judge's country house, seems to hear the final strains of Alice Pyncheon's ghostly harpsichord as she too leaves the House, floating heavenward.

Final and apparently effortless as these departures are, however, the old house still stands and is given the last words of the novel. For once the Author forsakes his alternate possibilities and says outright that Maule's Well throws up a kaleidoscope of pictures depicting the future family of Holgrave and Phoebe, and the Pyncheon elm whispers unintelligible prophecies. In other words, romance triumphs over realism in the end. The house and its legends endure even if its evil spell has been broken.

11

The Characters

Much of the critical discussion of *The House of the Seven Gables* has centered on the characters—and quite rightly so, since they are among the most striking ever created by Hawthorne. The symbolic and allegoric nature of *The House of the Seven Gables* has tempted critics to read into the five major characters, Hepzibah, Clifford, Phoebe, Holgrave, and Judge Pyncheon, all kinds of moral and psychological intentions. One of the most challenging theories, put forth by Martin Karlow,[1] is that Hawthorne was a precursor to the studies in schizophrenia by the famous twentieth-century psychologist, R. D. Laing. Karlow believes that *Seven Gables* is a study of the divided self. Judge Pyncheon represents the false self and Clifford the true self. Clifford is portrayed as infantile because as an infant he was never properly "embodied." He is split into a virtually distinct mind, "a forlorn inhabitant," and a decrepit body, "a ruinous mansion." The false self, the Judge, is portrayed as a facade, almost a caricature, of conventionality. From the moment that Clifford is introduced into the novel, we see his unreasonable fear of Jaffrey. This is, Karlow maintains, the true self's fear of envelopment by the false self. If once Jaffrey wins entry into the inner room of the house head, then Clifford will cease to exist.

The Characters

Clifford's desire to feel pain and to throw himself into the current of humanity is characteristic of the schizophrenic's desire to be born again as an ordinary human being. Karlow believes that Phoebe represents the best possibility of that rebirth. Through her Clifford begins to hear and smell and see. When she leaves the house she becomes the catalyst for a repetition of Clifford's primal loss of self and his breakdown.

In the death of Jaffrey, however, we see the murder of the false self. Clifford's consequent madness is a prologue to his recovery. The "Governor Pyncheon" chapter, with its elaborate portrayal of the death of the facade constitutes, in Langian terms, "the removal of the veil of the false self."

Holgrave, according to Karlow, represents another phase in the development of selfhood. Karlow points out their curious reversal of roles during the train episode. Holgrave appears to be paralyzed at the discovery of Jaffrey's body, while Clifford becomes the advocate of Holgrave's theories about the dead hand of the past to the fellow traveler on the train. They both return to reality when Phoebe gets back to the house. She rescues the two disembodied half-selves, Karlow claims, from their "being-beyond-the-world" (127).

In summary, Karlow proposes that *The House of the Seven Gables* is the story of Hawthorne's schizophrenia, his own twelve-year divorce from the world after leaving college, and his salvation and return to the real world through his marriage to his own Phoebe, Sophia.

Karlow's article is persuasive, even though he gets somewhat carried away by his own enthusiasm. It is not necessary, for example, to conclude, as he does, that the novel is "an example of schizophrenic form" because the book's "ostensible plot and its explicit moral are pretexts—a false-self system—for the hidden or subtle process—the true self" (Karlow, 123). The novel is not a pretext for anything; it is a multilayered, symbolic tale about the labyrinth of the human psyche, and, among many other things, a remarkably prophetic examination of the nature of schizophrenia.

Donald Junkins, in his essay on the novel, has a less radical explanation of four of the five major characters as prototypes for functions of the human mind. *The House of the Seven Gables* is, he claims, "a universal prototype of the process of individuation itself."[2] The house is a symbol of the whole mind; the four inhabitants are symbols of four basic psychological functions of the mind. The emergence of these characters from the house at the conclusion of the novel is a symbol of the process of individuation as it occurs in the regenerative human psyche.

With these symbolic functions in mind, Junkins sketches in the role of the four central characters tied to the house. Hepzibah, the sensitive and high-strung, faded gentlewoman, is totally oriented toward emotion. In contrast, Holgrave is oriented toward thinking; he is a writer, a scientist, a student and has a devouring intellectual curiosity. Phoebe is the opposite of Holgrave; she is no thinker, although she can think; she exudes light and joy; although she experiences emotions, she is not governed by them; she responds to sensuous perceptions of the world, but she is not directed by her senses. Compared to the other characters, Clifford undergoes the most change, according to Junkin. Beginning as an emotionally crippled man-child, he emerges from the house at the end a vigorous and aware adult.

Junkin moves from this analysis of the characters of the house to an examination of analogies with Hawthorne's personal life. Like Clifford and Holgrave, he claims, Hawthorne underwent a radical change in his life after his marriage to Sophia. The marriage and his resulting happiness released him from his self-incarceration in his own dungeon of the heart.

Junkin's theory weaves together the various threads of the novel and helps to justify its ending. A critic should always be wary, however, of tying a creative work too closely to biography. Moreover, the characters are too strongly individuated to be tied to specific psychological functions. Another flaw in the argument is that it does not take account of the central figure who does not live in the house but is so much a product of it, Jaffrey Pyncheon.

Richard Harter Fogle[3] also believes that only when the characters

The Characters

of *The House of the Seven Gables* are examined as a group do they
come properly alive. For him they operate only in relation to each
other and to the total design of the novel; in their time and place, the
characters are recognizable social, historical, and moral types. The
Judge is the modern reincarnation of "the Original Puritan," Hepzibah
"the aristocratic spinster," Clifford, "the inevitable product of material
success," Phoebe "the flower of New England," and Holgrave, "'the
new man,' American style . . . a sort of New England Mark Twain"
(Fogle, 113–14). For Fogle, it seems, the characters are far less individuals than symbolic functions.

The characters of *Seven Gables* have sparked a lot of critical interest because they are so interesting, but also, in my view, because
they are very original. It is possible to trace the influence of Charles
Dickens on the characterization—for example, we can note the sentimental Em'ly and Sophy of *David Copperfield* in Phoebe—but there
is little question that the major components of Hawthorne's characters
came out of his own observation of his New England neighbors and
his fertile imagination. For that reason, I cannot subscribe to the
views, discussed above, that the characters represent merely psychological functions or aspects of a whole personality. Eccentric, even
weird, as some of these characters are, they have about them the unmistakable ring of observed life.

HEPZIBAH

Hepzibah is the most memorable of the characters—the incarnation
of decayed gentility and eccentric spinsterhood, she is at once absurd,
comic, and pathetic. Hawthorne uses elements of caricature to portray
her, in her old turban and perpetual scowl. He repeatedly uses the
adjective "rusty" to describe her appearance and movements. Caricature gives way, however, to characterization as the novel proceeds
from portrait painting to interaction with others. A large part of
Hepzibah's problem is that she has lived for many years in almost total
isolation, which Holgrave calls "aloof, within your circle of gentility"

(44), or what Hawthorne often calls "the dungeon of the heart"—
which is the source of most of the problems his characters encounter.
When she is forced to open up commerce with the world, quite literally, in reopening the shop that her ancestor had opened a century
before in the old house, she is also forced to unbolt the locks on her
heart. This fall from gentility to commerce has its tragicomic aspects,
as Hawthorne indicates by his ironic references to the ghost of Ham-
let's father at the beginning of chapter 3 and Lady Macbeth's blood-
stained hands (51), but this change marks the beginning of her return
to psychic and even physical well-being.

Hawthorne also uses this incident to develop his thoughts about
democracy. He had read the work of the French Utopian, socialist
thinker, Charles Fourier, which indeed had influenced his decision to
enter the Brook Farm community. That experience soured him on
communal living, but it did not necessarily disillusion him about all
of the principles of equality and the distribution of wealth implicit in
Fourier's work. He had also read the work of another radical French
thinker, Pierre Proudhon, who believed that property was theft—an
idea that is the starting point of *Seven Gables*. Proudhon wanted to
replace capitalism with a system that would organize society into
groups that would bargain with each other over essential economic
and political issues within the framework of consensus about funda-
mental egalitarian principles.

In the chapter "Behind the Counter" Hawthorne demonstrates
how far American society is from these ideals. Hepzibah's first customer is an urchin, Ned Higgins, who is given a free gingerbread man
and immediately comes back for another. He wants, in fact, to exploit
an individual who out of generosity—and out of aristocratic reluc-
tance to go into trade—ignores the laws of a free market economy and
gives instead of barters. It is no accident, surely, that the gingerbread
man is Jim Crow, the colloquial, demeaning name for blacks. (This
name was applied to the infamous laws of some southern states,
which, after the Civil War, disregarded the Fourteenth Amendment
and denied blacks the same rights as whites.) The urchin unceremo-
niously swallows both Jim Crow gingerbread men. This is prob-

ably a comic but telling image of an oppressive caste and class society.

The gingerbread incident leads Hepzibah to change her mind about the class system, and she comes "to very disagreeable conclusions as to the temper and manners of what she termed the lower classes, whom, heretofore, she had looked down upon with a gentle and pitying complacence, as herself occupying a sphere of unquestionable superiority" (54–55). At the same time she finds herself fiercely resentful of the idle aristocracy to which she has herself recently belonged. Seeing an expensively dressed lady floating along the street, she wonders: "Must the whole world toil, that the palms of her hands may be kept white and delicate?" (55). Now in trade as well as desperately poor, she has a new, sour, view of the oppressive and discriminatory social system that keeps some idle while many toil and suffer.

It takes some time, therefore, for her to realize the truth in Holgrave's remark to her that in working for a living "you will at least have the sense of healthy and natural effort for a purpose, and of lending your strength—be it great or small—to the united struggle of mankind. This is success—all the success that anybody meets with!" (45).

She needs to make an effort to overcome her aversion to trade to gain the confidence to minister to the needs of her brother, who is broken physically and psychologically after thirty years in prison. She needs confidence particularly to resist the force and oppression of Judge Pyncheon who returns to haunt the House of the Seven Gables. She becomes almost heroic in her devotion to her brother's welfare. Hawthorne does not, however, dwell on these heroic qualities; he instead continually undercuts them by his mockery. Even in her most heroic gesture, her attempt to prevent Jaffrey Pyncheon from seeing Clifford, she is defeated. Despairing, she has to give way to the superior strength and determination of the Judge in his effort to wrest from Clifford what he believes to be the secret to the hidden wealth of the Pyncheons. In the end, however, her weakness defeats the Judge's apparent strength and justifies the meaning of her Hebraic name: "My delight is in her."

CLIFFORD

The characterization of Clifford is as remarkable in its different way as that of Hepzibah. He is, until the end of the novel, the child-man, reduced to impotence by hereditary weakness that has been exacerbated by his long prison term, all of which is compounded by the savage oppression and injustice visited upon him by his cousin Judge Pyncheon. He has been reduced to almost a ghost in the "ruinous mansion" (105) of his body, and of course in the house itself.

Seldom has the pathos of mental instability and incompetence been so well reproduced as in this portrait of Clifford. And yet, as with Hepzibah, Clifford's reentry into the world of humanity, his freedom from the literal dungeon, and then from the dungeon of the heart, signals the beginning of his painful rebirth. There is a material and sensual aspect to this reentry as when he gorges himself on the breakfast his sister prepares for him and drinks cup after cup of the fragrant coffee. He also casts more than an appreciative and avuncular eye on Phoebe's sexual attractions.

There is also a spiritual aspect to his rebirth, which is nourished by the aesthetic appeal of Phoebe's charms and by beautiful objects, especially flowers. Ugliness is mortifying to him, as Hepzibah discovers to her chagrin. In spite of all the loving care and attention she lavishes on him, her brother can scarcely bear to look at her.

Modern psychology has called Clifford's condition schizophrenia: a radical disjunction of personality. He alternates between frenzied activity and utter torpor. Sometimes he masochistically begs for pain so that he can feel that he is alive, as when he asks Phoebe for a rose so that he may press its thorns into his flesh; at another time he has to be forcibly restrained from throwing himself over the edge of the balcony of the arched window from which he is watching a parade. "He needed a shock," Hawthorne comments, "or perhaps he required to take a deep, deep plunge into the ocean of human life, and to sink down and be covered by its profoundness, and then to emerge, sobered, invigorated, restored to the world and to himself" (166). Such a shock is provided after Clifford discovers the body of Jaf-

The Characters

frey Pyncheon and flees the house with Hepzibah. The escape arouses all of Clifford's dormant energies into a kind of fever of activity. He and his sister are drawn at last "into the great current of human life" (256) when, for the first time, they board a train. Hepzibah's imagination is still stuck fast in the House of the Seven Gables where she has spent so much of her life, but Clifford is transported literally and metaphorically. To a testy fellow traveler he launches into an encomium of trains as an emblem of a future state of happiness—an escape from "these heaps of bricks and stones" (261) that men call house and home. His lyrical eulogy of modern scientific thought, including mesmerism and electricity, is, however, quickly deflated when the testy traveler reminds him that the telegraph can convey not only thoughts of love from Maine to Florida, but also news of fleeing murderers.

Reminded of the body in the old house, Clifford grabs Hepzibah and they leave the train at the next stop. Their return to grim reality is symbolized by a ruined church and farmhouse close to the wayside station. Dragged down to torpidity once again, Clifford can only beg Hepzibah to take the lead. All she can do is pray for God's mercy.

PHOEBE

The leavening agent in this heavy tale is Phoebe, who has been the subject of much critical discussion. The biographical source for her is obvious: Hawthorne's wife, Sophia, had been instrumental in rescuing him from his spiritual and physical isolation and opening up for him a commerce with the world. She was of a sunny disposition, incurably optimistic, an admirable housekeeper and flower arranger and, like Phoebe, small in body. Moreover, she had urged him to write a brighter book after he had completed the dark and terrible *The Scarlet Letter*. His pet name for her was Phoebe, the small, darting, singing bird common to New England.

The literary origins of Phoebe are also clear. Her prototype is the fair lady of romance tradition, domesticated and sentimentalized by nineteenth-century melodrama. For Hawthorne she is also a symbol

95

of that democratic renewal and energy of the common people that he saw as the transforming agent of the ancestral, aristocratic, and decaying past. She is no thinker, but an active busy housewife who has the knack, like the good fairy, of transforming her surroundings by her presence and disposition. In the novel, she is associated strongly with nature, "as graceful as a bird," Hawthorne writes, "as pleasant, about the house, as a gleam of sunshine falling on the floor through a shadow of twinkling leaves, or as a ray of firelight that dances on the wall, while evening is drawing nigh" (80).

These qualities transform the atmosphere of the House of the Seven Gables: the grime vanishes, the dry rot is stayed, the shadows and the scent of death are banished. Phoebe is the unfallen Eve who restores to Clifford the possibility of life and even happiness. He gazes on her beauty, listens to the sweet sound of her voice, and takes sustenance from her reality. For her part, she is sometimes oppressed by the heavy atmosphere of the house and by Clifford's temperament, but she is loath to explore the riddle of his spiritual and physical enervation and refuses to reflect on it. She is content to tend him and the house and garden so that he can avoid the harsh thoughts of his past, and live in the pleasures of the present.

Phoebe is too good to be true, and Hawthorne is aware that he is sometimes stretching the credulity of his reader in his way of representing her. To justify this minute and sentimental treatment of the minutiae of household life and domestic attentions, he falls back on biblical story and allegory to justify his method. "It was the Eden of a thunder-smitten Adam," he continues, "who had fled for refuge thither out of the same dreary and perilous wilderness, into which the original Adam was expelled" (150). Only when Phoebe returns to her parents' home for a visit is the Edenic blessing suspended, and sin and death can again enter the House of the Seven Gables in the person of Jaffrey Pyncheon.

The Characters

HOLGRAVE

Although he lives in one of the seven gables, Holgrave is a strangely peripheral figure for most of the action of the novel. He is mentioned early on as the first customer to visit Hepzibah's cent-shop, and he reappears again briefly in chapter 6, "Maule's Well," as indeed he should, being a Maule. His identity as such, however, is kept concealed—a Gothic secret—until almost the end of the novel. In effect, he does not make a full appearance until more than halfway through the novel, in chapter 12, "The Daguerreotypist." There Hawthorne gives him a history as well as a name, and a kind of symbolic identity as Young America. Born of poor parents, with little education, he has knocked about the world and practiced almost a dozen occupations. He is the reincarnation of Benjamin Franklin's Poor Richard. His further symbolic identity is established by his having been a Yankee pedlar, a legendary figure whose origins are in the satirical sketches of Sam Slick, a pedlar created by the nineteenth-century Canadian author T. C. Haliburton.

Holgrave is a child of the nineteenth century, having been a member of a socialist community (the hippie communes of the period), and a practicer of mesmerism, a form of hypnosis. Jack-of-all-trades, wanderer, incipient anarchist, he is in a sense outside of society, which is probably why Hawthorne kept him essentially off the scene until late in the book. Holgrave stands for youth, spiritual inexperience, impatience. This is why there is a good deal of wistful irony in Hawthorne's reflection that Holgrave is "the representative of many compeers in his native land" (181). The phrase is reminiscent of Emerson's essay "Representative Men," and, as F. O. Matthiessen has asserted, Holgrave is an ironic commentary on Emersonian optimism (Matthiessen, 331). Holgrave, too, at least until he encounters the dead body of the Judge, is Emerson's self-reliant man, confident of the future and scornful of the past. Holgrave's soliloquy about the past could be taken as a commentary on Emerson's address, "The American Scholar." He utters this condemnation of the past in his harangue to Phoebe in chapter 12. It is perhaps the eternal cry of the young against the authority of their elders and against the weight of the past, and it is uttered with deep emotion:

> We read in Dead Men's books! We laugh at Dead Men's jokes, and cry at Dead Men's pathos! We are sick of Dead Men's diseases, physical and moral, and die of the same remedies with which dead doctors killed their patients! We worship the living Deity, according to Dead Men's forms and creeds! Whatever we seek to do, of our own free motion, a Dead Man's icy hand obstructs us! Turn our eyes to what point we may, a Dead Man's white, immitigable face encounters them, and freezes our very heart! And we must be dead ourselves, before we can begin to have our proper influence on our own world, which will then be no longer of our world, but the world of another generation, with which we shall have no shadow of a right to interfere. I ought to have said, too, that we live in Dead Men's houses; as, for instance, in this of the seven gables! (183)

This sentiment is surely at the root of most revolutions and other profound social changes—a radical impatience with things as they are, which seem merely to be things as they always have been. There is a reflection of this philosophy even in the story he tells Phoebe, in "Alice Pyncheon." Holgrave's ancestor, Matthew Maule, will have nothing to do with the expected forms of the hierarchical society of the time, which is the mid-eighteenth century. As a tradesman, he is expected to go to the back door, "where servants and work-people were usually admitted" (191). The black slave, Scipio (the Jim Crow of the period), who admits him mumbles, "Lord-a-Mercy, what a great man he be, this carpenter fellow! . . . Anybody think he beat on the door with his biggest hammer!" (192). Even in a period that allowed the most blatant expression of the class system and slavery—which was not abolished in New England until 1779, after the American Revolution— Maule is not prepared to acknowledge rank in his behavior toward "the worshipful" Gervase Pyncheon. Pyncheon, on the other hand, takes care to address Maule by the title "Goodman," which indicates Maule's low social status. There is a strong class resentment, as well as a hereditary quarrel, in Maule's revenge on Pyncheon.

The Characters

Holgrave goes beyond attacking the reign of the dead and the class system: he also attacks the root ideas of a conservative, capitalist society—tradition, succession, and property. He wants to destroy not only houses with each generation but also all public buildings—state houses, city halls, and churches—for they symbolize the permanence of ideas as well as institutions. Further, he wants to change the institution of the family, the central form and tradition of society. "To plant a family!" he exclaims. "This idea is at the bottom of most of the wrong and mischief which men do. The truth is, that, once in every half-century, at longest, a family should be merged into the great, obscure mass of humanity, and forget all about its ancestors" (185). He holds up the various lunacies of the Pyncheon family as examples of the truth of his argument.

Phoebe takes an eminently commonsense view of these heresies. To his proposal that we should not live in Dead Men's houses, she simply replies, "And why not . . . so long as we can be comfortable in them?" (183). She adds later that it makes her dizzy to think of living in the shifting world that would result if Holgrave's radical views were carried out.

Hawthorne is more ambivalent about Holgrave than he is about any of the other characters in the novel; and it is an ambivalence that goes to the root of the democratic, capitalistic system of the United States. "There appeared to be qualities in Holgrave," the Author comments, "such as, in a country where everything is free to the hand that can grasp it, could hardly fail to put some of the world's prizes within his reach. But these matters are delightfully uncertain" (181). In a democracy like this, freedom to rise has to be accompanied by the freedom to fail; and promise is by no means a guarantee of achievement. The author continues his generalizations:

> At almost every step in life, we meet with young men of just about Holgrave's age, for whom we anticipate wonderful things, but of whom, even after much and careful inquiry, we never happen to hear another word. The effervescence of youth and passion, and the fresh gloss of the intellect and imagination, endow them with a false

brilliancy, which makes fools of themselves and other people. Like certain chintzes, calicoes, and ginghams, they show finely in their first newness, but cannot stand the sun and rain, and assume a very sober aspect after washing-day. (181)

This is a highly unflattering portrait of his hero, the metaphors of which are revealing. They relate to the manufacture of cheap and shoddy industrial soft goods, made for show and not for durability. They are in fact products of what used to be called "the five and dime store." A consumer society, which the United States was in the process of becoming, depends on such products to keep the economy going. Hawthorne is making an analogy between this consumer process and Holgrave's rootlessness and constantly changing occupations. Holgrave's situation reflects the complete opposite of the condition of a stable, aristocratic society, in which occupation and status are fairly well fixed and objects are produced with art and craftsmanship, for durability not mere consumption.

Holgrave's present occupation as a daguerreotypist is a perfect metaphor for his identity. It puts him at the forefront of the contemporary technology of taking photographic portraits—as opposed to the previous painstaking method of oil painting. The photograph rapidly became another consumer good and an emblem of the transience it captures so well. Daguerreotype is used skillfully by Hawthorne not only to define Holgrave's occupation and nature but to define other characters as well.

Daguerreotype photographs were made by taking a specially treated silver-surfaced plate and exposing it to the subject and developing it with the fumes from mercury. After five minutes or more, depending upon the intensity of the light, an image formed upon the plate. As Holgrave himself says to Phoebe, "I make pictures out of sunshine." He adds, "There is a wonderful insight in heaven's broad and simple sunshine. While we give it credit only for depicting the merest surface, it actually brings out the secret character with a truth no painter would ever venture upon, even could he detect it" (91). The daguerreotype portrait could be said to reveal truth because the length of the exposure made it imperative for the subject's head to be held still in a clamp for many minutes; and it is difficult to maintain a posed and artificial expression for that length of time. Holgrave shows Phoebe a photograph that she first mistakes for her ancestor in the picture on the wall, but Holgrave assures her that it is the image of her living cousin, the Judge. He points out that although the Judge wears in the world's eye a pleasant, sunny, benevolent countenance, the sun has brought out in the daguerreotype the real man: "sly, subtle, hard, imperious, and, withal, cold as ice" (92). Holgrave, like his photographic method, is a truth teller; and one of his roles in the novel is to reveal hidden knowledge to other characters.

Hawthorne as Author also comments on Holgrave's philosophy and indicates how far he himself has moved from his earlier days of communitarian idealism. Noting that Holgrave's ideas would inevitably be modified by advancing years, he adds that "the haughty faith, with which [Holgrave] began life, would be well bartered for a far humbler one, at its close, in discerning that man's best-directed effort accomplishes a kind of dream, while God is the sole worker of realities" (180). This is an expression of Christian quietism that is getting perilously close to an attitude of complacency, or even apathy.

Later on, Phoebe gets to the heart of what Hawthorne seems to consider Holgrave's fallacies by pointing out his lack of bonds to the human community. Holgrave has lost touch with the rub, trouble, and joy of family life. Phoebe is right when she accuses him of looking on the drama of the House of Pyncheon as the spectator of a tragedy and on the old house itself as a theater. This isolation has its benefits artistically since it makes Holgrave analogous to the choric figure in Greek drama.

Holgrave is also that familiar figure in Hawthorne's early stories and *The Scarlet Letter,* the thinker, the scientist, the cold-hearted speculator. This aspect of his character is reflected in his name, which means "son of the grave"—a name that also prefigures his resurrection after his encounter with the body of the Judge. He has some of the Maule traits that have made them vulnerable to accusations of witchcraft. Even his photography is a means of using the Maule gifts of second sight. By photographing the Judge unawares, for example, Holgrave can penetrate his hypocritical mask and reveal the true evil beneath. In a conversation with Phoebe about Clifford he tells her that had he her opportunities for observation, "no scruples would prevent me from fathoming Clifford to the full extent of my plummet-line!" (178). When he tells the tale of Alice Pyncheon to Phoebe, he induces in her a trancelike state and perceives that it would be easy to establish domination over her spirit. Unlike his ancestor Matthew Maule, however, he resists the temptation and releases her from the spell. He renounces his visionary powers when he realizes that they are simply too dangerous. He has, too, amid all his changes of occupation, retained his integrity; and he is learning, through his growing affection for Phoebe, to leave his cold, isolated position and participate more sympathetically in the affairs of society. His union with Phoebe starts him on the road to the conservative attitude that he articulates at the end of the novel.

JUDGE JAFFREY PYNCHEON

Integrity and affection are not qualities possessed by Judge Pyncheon, who is the Pyncheon inheritance incarnate. As Holgrave says, "the original perpetrator and father of this mischief appears to have perpetuated himself, and still walks the street . . . with the fairest prospect of transmitting to posterity as rich, and as wretched, an inheritance as he has received!" (185). The Judge is the emblem of prosperous hypocrisy. With his rich clothes, his gold-headed cane, and his dignified bearing, he apparently represents the father figure: respectable, responsible, authoritative; but he is actually the false father, a father of evil, a Satanic figure.

Hawthorne spends a good deal of time editorially discussing what he calls "the solid unrealities" of Pyncheon's life, for Hawthorne was fascinated by the problem of power and authority. Pyncheon to him was typical of a whole class of men who treasure form over substance and spend their lives in building up hoards of gold and quantities of real estate. From this base they seek political office and public honors. For the Judge the idea of family takes second place to the dream of wealth. He apparently achieves the release of Clifford, whom he had framed and then convicted for killing their uncle Jaffrey, not out of any sense of guilt but because Clifford would then be more accessible and more easily forced to reveal the whereabouts of the fabled riches of the Pyncheons.

When he confronts Hepzibah in chapter 15, "The Scowl and the Smile," the Judge lays it on the line when he tells her that it was one of Uncle Jaffrey's eccentricities to conceal his great wealth by making foreign investments, perhaps under assumed names, "and by various means, familiar enough to capitalists, but unnecessary here to be specified" (234). These foreign investments were undoubtedly the nineteenth-century versions of numbered Swiss bank accounts.

Judge Pyncheon is not only the emblem of grasping, selfish, capitalism, he is also unable to believe that any way of looking at life other than his own has any value. "I do not belong to the dreaming class of men," he tells Hepzibah (235), and yet his life is lived in dreaming of wealth that is more illusory than even the shadowy lives of Hepzibah and Clifford. He has, as the narrator remarks, the Midas touch, a gift with consequences that prove fatal, as the myth tells us.

THE HOUSE

When all is said and done, the House of the Seven Gables is the chief character in the book, as well as its structural and thematic center. On the first page of the book the Author tells us that "the venerable mansion has always affected me like a human countenance, bearing the traces not merely of outward storm and sunshine, but expressive also of the long lapse of mortal life, and accompanying vicissitudes, that have passed within" (5). The house has a heart as well as a face: "So much of mankind's various experience had passed there . . . that the very timbers were oozy, as with the moisture of a heart. It was itself like a great human heart, with a life of its own, and full of rich and sombre reminiscences" (27). Whenever Hawthorne mentions the human heart, he intends moral ambiguities. The heart is the seat of not only the emotion of love, but also all the other less admirable emotions too; it is therefore not surprising that Hawthorne often called the heart the dungeon: it can, by harboring the emotions of pride and envy lock the possessor into isolation. Moreover, these emotions released in passion from the dungeon could wreak terrible havoc on others.

The heart of the house is at least temporarily lightened by the advent of Phoebe. The window-eyes show this change: "It really seemed as if the battered visage of the House . . . , black and heavy-browed as it still certainly looked, must have shown a kind of cheerfulness glimmering through its dusky windows, as Phoebe passed to-and-fro in the interior" (81). But the heaviness of the house takes its toll even on the lightsome Phoebe. Her experience there becomes more important to her than anything she had experienced before. Every object in the house "responded to her consciousness, as if a moist human heart were in it" (219). The house predictably has an even greater effect on its long-time denizen, Hepzibah, who incarnates it more than any of the other characters. Even when she leaves it to take the train ride with Clifford, she cannot escape it. Varied scenes rush past the train window, but she can see only "the seven old gable-peaks. . . . This one old house was everywhere!" (258).

When Judge Pyncheon dies, the house comes alive as never before. It wrestles with the wind of the storm and bellows with its sooty throat—its wide chimney. It sings and sighs and sobs and shrieks—"A rumbling kind of a bluster roars behind the fire-board" (277). All in all, the House of the Seven Gables is an emblem of the unregenerate heart of man, full of envy, wrath, pride, lust, and the other deadly sins; this is why the other characters are so happy to escape from it at the end of the tale.

CHARACTER AND THEME

Each character has an organic, historic connection with the house; the destinies of each, in different ways, have been shaped, or distorted, by it. Hawthorne obviously intends some kind of analogical tie, which is at least as much historical as it is psychological. Each of us is a product of our past, hereditarily and historically. Some people become dominated by their past, as are Hepzibah and Clifford. They are examples and victims of the colonial and aristocratic views of life outmoded in the nineteenth century.

The novel is making the point that unless we escape from the past and accept our common, democratic, yet independent lot, we remain shackled to it. Unless we escape from the past, both historical and parental, we remain in a state, as it were, of perpetual infancy; we can never become fully individuated or fully mature, free human beings.

12

Structure, Style, and Emblem and Symbol

STRUCTURE

A glance at the table of contents of *The House of the Seven Gables* reveals that Hawthorne for the most part uses scenic episodes interspersed with static portraits of his major characters to structure his novel. In some chapters he combines static portraiture with dramatic action. The first chapter, "The Old Pyncheon Family," is both a group portrait of the Pyncheons and the Maules and the house that they built together and a dramatization of the original opening of the house and the death of the Colonel. The next chapter, "The Little Shop Window," is in essence a portrait of Hepzibah, and the following one, "A Day behind the Counter," a dramatization of her new occupation as shopkeeper. So the novel proceeds, not as a continuous narrative but as a series of building blocks that all contribute to the cumulative effect of character and action. The most important portrait chapters, symbolically, are "The Daguerreotypist" and "Governor Pyncheon." The first presents an image of democratic man, and the second an ironic image of privilege—wealth and power—all frustrated by the great leveler, death.

Structure, Style, and Emblem and Symbol

It has often been said that Hawthorne is poor at structure, that all of his best works, even *The Scarlet Letter,* are short narratives. True, he is not a master of long, continuous narrative, as are Dickens, Thackeray, and Henry James. Perhaps realizing this, he makes a virtue of necessity and makes full use of alternating picture and scene to build *The House of the Seven Gables.* In addition he makes use of other structural devices, particularly thematic repetition, an organic style, allegorical devices, and symbolism, to achieve unity in the novel.

One of the fascinations of *The House of the Seven Gables* is tracing the variations on the theme of the artist and the artistic process—often expressed in musical terms. When Holgrave is entertaining company in the garden, the Author comments, "Either it was one of those up-quivering flashes of the spirit, to which minds in an abnormal state are liable; or else the artist had subtly touched some chord that made musical vibration" (157). Phoebe's song continually floats through the house or comes "inward from the garden, with the twinkling sunbeams" (138). Then there is the ghostly sound of Alice Pyncheon's harpsichord, the echo of a dead past. Hawthorne also mentions "the solemn symphony, that rolled its undertone through Hepzibah's and her brother's life" (139).

Darrel Abel has claimed that the symphonic analogy is also a structural principle. He considers the book "not as a narrative organized by strict concatenation of events, but as a kind of prose symphony organized in five stages or movements."[1] The unifying theme in this symphony, according to Abel, is the long continuance of the House of the Seven Gables, which, Hawthorne says at the beginning of the book, if worthily recounted, "would form a narrative of no small interest and instruction, and possessing, moreover, a certain remarkable unity" (5).

The first movement, says Abel, establishes the House as "a projection of human ideas, an expression of tradition" (257). Nature seems friendly to this tradition. The Pyncheon elm hangs over it: "It gave beauty to the old edifice, and seemed to make it a part of nature" (27).

The second movement, "concerns the building of the House (establishment of tradition) and the defining of human relationships involved in its building" (Abel, 259). In the construction of the house the original crimes of theft and judicial murder were also built in, as well as the historical relationship of enmity between the Pyncheons and the Maules.

The third movement "represents the House in apparent prosperity still, but actually in incipient decay" (Abel, 261). The Pyncheons as a family are undergoing decay, like the house itself. As depicted in Holgrave's story of Gervase Pyncheon, the covetousness of the original Pyncheons has persisted and the carnality of the Colonel has become the "refined sybaritism" of Gervase. The old pride of the Pyncheons has become condescending haughtiness in Alice. Yet there is still some beauty and grace in the aristocratic tradition even though it has lost vitality. Abel should also have added that there has been a decline in the Maule family too. The democratic pride of the original Maule has become surliness in Matthew, and the curse has become murderous.

The fourth movement of the novel, according to Abel, "represents tradition in an advanced state of dilapidation" (Abel, 263). The House is falling apart; the Maules have lapsed into obscurity; Gervase's rapacity has become the Judge's mania, and Gervase's sybaritism Clifford's imbecility. Alice's aristocratic pride has become Hepzibah's absurd pretensions. But Alice's womanly feelings have found a new, more wholesome expression in Phoebe. The hypnotic powers of the Maules have passed to Holgrave and are transformed in him to beneficial and artistic ends.

Abel claims that the fifth movement is "the climactic continuation of the fourth" (Abel, 263). Within the house are assembled the elements of vitality and wholesomeness that have been missing since its founding. The tradition is renovated through the transformation of Phoebe, who is not a lady but is, Hawthorne writes, "the example of feminine grace and availability combined, in a state of society, if there were any such, where ladies did not exist" (80). She is compared to the ridiculous Hepzibah as "new Plebeianism" as against "old Gentility" (80–81). Phoebe banishes the grime and decay of the old house. Even nature around the house is transformed by her presence. "Phoebe as woman, then," Abel concludes, "not as Pyncheon, and Holgrave as man, not as Maule, are reconciled in the moonlight in the garden (Abel, 265). The transforming power of love renovates and transforms the house and its traditions. Abel comments on the ineptness of the neatly tied up ending of the novel, in which the lucky survivors are "left in comfortable enjoyment of [Judge Pyncheon's] ill-gotten wealth" (Abel, 267). But he justifies the conclusion as a fictional demonstration of Hawthorne's conviction that "any distinct stream of human existence cannot be scrutinized in individual lives . . . [but] must be examined in larger configurations in which a succession of lives exhibits the prolonged development of human tendencies" (Abel, 268). The novel is thus an allegory of "love versus self-love, of human tradition versus personal ambition and family pride, of imagination versus preoccupation with present fact" (Abel, 268).

STYLE

The style of the novel is linked closely to the structural elements of picture and scene. The dramatic scenes proceed largely by dialogue, the style of which does much to establish the characters. The best example of this is found in chapter 17, "The Flight of Two Owls." The picture chapters use descriptive techniques that focus on details of dress and expression and also draw on the picturesque style of painting popular during Hawthorne's time.

The picturesque style often used ruins and emblematic figures to present a moral lesson about the effects of time and change. Hawthorne employs the technique to dramatize a decaying aristocratic society in describing the house in chapter 1. He emphasizes the old elm tree, the blackened roof, the ruinous fence and abundant weeds surrounding the house, and the straggling flowers of Alice's posies.

> The tradition was, that a certain Alice Pyncheon had flung up the
> seeds, in sport, and that the dust of the street and the decay of the
> roof gradually formed a kind of soil for them, out of which they

grew, when Alice had long been in her grave. However the flowers might have come there, it was both sad and sweet to observe how Nature adopted to herself this desolate, decaying, gusty, rusty, old house of the Pyncheon family; and how the ever-returning Summer did her best to gladden it with tender beauty, and grew melancholy with the effort. (28)

Not only are humankind and nature treated in the typically romantic fashion in respect to the passing of time and the glorification of the processes of the natural world, but also the very diction is typical of the romantic style. Words and phases like "desolate," "ever-returning Summer," "tender beauty," and "melancholy" are typical of romantic poetry, particularly that of Keats and Shelley. Both Nature and Summer are personified. A number of poetic devices contribute to this rhythmic and melodic prose: alliteration, "seeds in sport," "dust . . . and . . . decay," "sad and sweet," "desolate, decaying"; and assonance, such as "flung . . . dust"; even rhyme, "gusty, rusty." The punctuation, which consists of many more commas and other marks than in modern prose, tends to slow down the pace of the sentence, emphasizing its melancholy and reflective mood. The syntax is also generally more complex than that found in most modern narratives. In the typical excerpt quoted above the first sentence is compound, with the coordinate conjunction "and"; and complex, with a subordinate clause introduced by "when" in the second half of the compound sentence. The second sentence is even more complicated syntactically. It is introduced by a subordinate clause, "However," and has three independent clauses, the last two, each introduced by "and," balancing the first one. And yet, so sure is Hawthorne's command of rhythm and sentence structure, so clear is the direction in which he is moving in this sentence and in the remainder of the paragraph and the next, that there is no sign of strain or artificiality—yet the sentence is full of artifice. The art is to conceal art.

The style is organic, another characteristic of the romantic tradition. That is to say, the images of graves, rust, decay, and dust connect with the theme of decline and death in the novel; on the other hand, the images of flowers, soil, summer, and beauty connect with the theme of growth, renewal, and life.

As in so many other aspects of the novel, however, Hawthorne parodies this style by going on to describe the shop door cut into the old house, which, he says, "we greatly fear, may damage any picturesque and romantic impression, which we have been willing to throw over our sketch of this respectable edifice" (28). There is even internal parody in the section quoted above. The word "gusty" does not really belong to this romantic set piece; it is a word too kinetic, too comic for the context.

This process of self-parody, or parodying the conventions of romantic and Gothic writing, goes on all the time in the novel. After picturesquely describing the ruinous state of Maule's Well, for example, Hawthorne immediately embarks on a comic description of the degenerate chickens in their coop beside the well. Stylistically as well as thematically, Hawthorne consistently undercuts high seriousness and aristocratic pretension.

EMBLEM AND SYMBOL

Another notable feature of Hawthorne's style is his frequent use of emblem and symbol. In his employment of the emblem, Hawthorne was heavily influenced by the Puritan tradition, in which the whole world is emblematic of God's presence. The early Puritans in North America frequently resorted to emblem books with which they translated the meaning of external reality. There are many traditional emblems in *Seven Gables,* including the sword, the garden, the flower, the mirror, the tree, and the fountain. Hawthorne also adapts this tradition to his own use by making the emblem take on symbolic value, increasing the resonance, and often the irony, of the sign. An example of this is the bloody ruff of Colonel Pyncheon as he sits dead in his chair. The ruff is symbolic both of his status and his violent death. The ruff has a further analogy in the halter pictured around the neck of Matthew Maule just before his death, when he prophesies that God will give Pyncheon blood to drink. This bloody ruff is echoed in the bloodstain across the "snowy neckcloth" (280) of Judge Pyncheon when the time comes for him to die in the same way as his ancestor.

Another symbolic use of clothing in the novel is Hepzibah's turban, which is a parody on the headgear used by a powerful sultan. Her headgear is further parodied by the scanty crest of the degenerate chickens, "so oddly and wickedly analogous," Hawthorne points out, "to Hepzibah's turban" (89). Hepzibah also wears rusty black gowns in contrast to Phoebe's virginal white ones. Clifford inveterately wears an old faded demask dressing gown, a pitiable remnant of the rich gown it had once been. In contrast, Holgrave wears cheap, ordinary, simple clothing, supplied by a Boston department store.

The overarching symbol in the book is the house itself, frequently compared not only to the history of the Pyncheon and Maule families, but also to Hepzibah and Clifford in its decay, rustiness, scowling windows, and dry rot. In contrast to the sterility and decay of the house, a stream of daily life flows by its arched window under the fascinated gaze of Clifford, who is tempted to plunge in, as he does later in the railroad chapter.

It must be remembered, however, that there are two other houses in the book: the thatched hut by a pure spring belonging to Matthew Maule, his "garden-ground and homestead," and Judge Pyncheon's elegant wooden country house. The first house seems to hark back to a kind of golden age of pastoral simplicity. Colonel Pyncheon destroys this house and erects over it the House of the Seven Gables, inaugurating an Iron Age of greed and power. The house is emblematic of not only the seven deadly sins, but also, in time, the stricken heart of the Pyncheon family. Only after Clifford and Hepzibah have fled this house on the death of the Judge and have taken the railroad journey, thus discovering the present and the future, can this old house be left forever. They, and Phoebe and Holgrave, revealed as the last of the Maules, can now move into the country house that has devolved to them through the Judge's death.

13

The Problem of the Conclusion

The death of Judge Jaffrey Pyncheon precipitates the conclusion—a conclusion endlessly debated by the critics. The death has been made the subject of an investigation by a critic-detective, Alfred H. Marks, who points the finger of accusation first at Hawthorne himself.[1] "No murder," he writes, "was ever planned so calculatedly as was Judge Pyncheon's demise in this novel. He died as full of gore and as close to the scene of many of his crimes as were Penelope's suitors when Odysseus slew them" (Marks, 414). The Judge's death is, Marks says, the revenge of imagination over the power of economic materialism and Philistinism. Hawthorne's agent in the crime, is Clifford, the lover of the beautiful. The chair that the Judge dies in is the same one that Clifford inveterately occupies for his morning naps, and has thus been made the seat of the imagination, antipathetic to the Judge's iron materialism. More to the point, though, when Hepzibah goes in search of her brother, whose presence has been commanded by the Judge, she finds him, finally, not in his bedroom or anywhere else in the house but coming out of the room in which the body sits. Marks theorizes that Clifford would never have gone into that room if he had known that the Judge was there, but has gone for his customary nap and discovers the Judge sitting in his chair; we do not know whether or not the Judge was still alive when Clifford came upon him.

Marks also points to Hawthorne's rhetorical question when the Judge sinks wearily into the chair to await Clifford: "Was it a little matter—a trifle, to be prepared for in a single moment, and to be rested from, in another moment—that he must now, after thirty years, encounter a kinsman risen from a living tomb, and wrench a secret from him, or else consign him to a living tomb again?" (238). When Hepzibah sees Clifford emerging from the death chamber, she notes that his face is preternaturally white, deadly white, so that Hepzibah can discern his features in the dim hallway "as if a light fell on them alone." This must have been the face that Clifford presented to the Judge, eerily disembodied, which might have been the shock required to bring on the apoplexy that killed him. This reaction would be a fitting and ironic end for a man who has claimed never to mistake shadow for substance.

We can never know whether Hawthorne intended this inference to be taken from the death of the Judge, as it is compassed around with his usual ambiguity. Such a death would, however, be congruent with Hawthorne's irony throughout the novel. The cause of death is given further validation by another circumstance not mentioned by Marks. When the old gentleman in the train remarks that the electric telegraph can be used to detect bank robbers and murderers, Clifford replies that he does not like that point of view and adds that murderers often "deserve to be ranked among public benefactors" (265). Soon afterwards, acting like a guilty man under the suspicious gaze of the old traveler, he leaves the train at a wayside station, his effervescence quite extinguished.

Clifford has reason to be fearful, of course, having been sent to prison before for a crime he did not commit. But this time there are no witnesses, false or otherwise. Clifford's part in the death, if any, escapes detection, except by literary critics. Certain it is that the death has "a permanently invigorating and ultimately beneficial effect on Clifford" (313). The nightmare of the Judge's presence has been lifted and Clifford rises from his apathy to live, within his limited physical means, happily.

The Problem of the Conclusion

Many people say, too (as Hawthorne puts it in his customary ambiguous way), that the daguerreotypist obtains from a mesmeric seer the truth about the death of old Jaffrey Pyncheon—that it was caused not by Clifford, but by an apoplectic seizure at the sight of his young reprobate and dissolute cousin, Jaffrey, rifling the drawers of his desk. If we accept Alfred Marks's theory, this death is strangely similar to the one suffered later by Judge Jaffrey himself. Young Jaffrey, after the death of old Jaffrey, coolly continued to search the drawers, destroyed the will made out in Clifford's favor, and left in place an earlier one favoring him. Then he falsified the evidence so that the guilt for the break-in, and the subsequent death, fell on Clifford.

So Clifford regains at last his shattered reputation, although, as the Author sententiously points out, "After such wrong as he had suffered, there is no reparation. . . . [N]o great mistake, whether acted or endured, in our moral sphere, is ever really set right" (313). This ending reaffirms the theme of the novel that the sins of the fathers are visited "upon the children unto the third and fourth generation." This moral undercuts the happy note on which the novel ends.

The Judge's death is no less fortunate for all the other characters, because through his death, and the fortuitous death of his only son in Europe, Hepzibah and Phoebe, as well as Clifford, become rich. Through Phoebe, Holgrave also hits the jackpot. Not only that: through his love for Phoebe Holgrave is transformed from a wild-eyed reformer, despiser of the past, and hater of property to a landowner and conservative who laments that the Judge's country house is built not of stone but of wood! He reveals himself to everyone as a descendant of the wizard Maule and touches the spring that Clifford had long ago also dreamily discovered, which reveals the secret niche in which the now useless deed to the Maine lands has rested for nearly two hundred years. The old Colonel's picture crashes to the ground. Released from its spell, the united Pyncheons and Maules leave the House of the Seven Gables forever in a "handsome, dark-green barouche,"—the contemporary version of the Cadillac—accompanied by the chorus-figure Uncle Venner, who will become the group's armchair philosopher. The choral role is taken over by some bystanders, one of whom comments that Old Maid Pyncheon has done pretty well by her cent-shop investment. He adds, "if we are to take it as the will of Providence, why, I can't exactly fathom it!" (318).

Maule's Well is throwing up its kaleidoscopic pictures, foreshadowing a happy future for the descendants of the Maules and Pyncheons, while Uncle Venner seems to hear the final strains of Alice Pyncheon's harpsichord as she floats heavenward from the old house.

Many critics have been discomfited by this outcome because this is the only one of all of Hawthorne's novels to end on such an overwhelmingly positive note. The lovers are reunited, the plot's complications are resolved, the virtuous are rewarded and the wicked are punished. William Charvat, in his introduction to the *Centenary Edition* of the novel, has gone so far as to maintain that Hawthorne had not intended this ending at all: "What he poured over it may be called sunshine, perhaps, but it was no part of his original plan, if, indeed, he had planned this conclusion at all."[2] Marcus Cunliffe, on the other hand, asserts that the ending was done according to plan: "Hawthorne," he writes, "traced the ramifications of his germinal idea with scrupulous care. We never feel that he has taken himself by surprise, any more than he expects or attempts to surprise the reader."[3] Some critics maintain that Hawthorne wrapped it up in this way to please his wife, after her negative reaction to the darkness of *The Scarlet Letter*. Others have said that he so arranged the ending to record his happy marriage. Yet others conclude that he was courting the mid–nineteenth century American popular audiences, eager then, as now, for happy endings.

Frederick Crews's psychoanalytical reading of the novel, discussed earlier, posits that this killing of the father figure and the happy outcome of the plot is an Oedipal wish fulfillment and an avoidance of the real issue of hereditary guilt and punishment. In support of this thesis, Crews points to the vindictive pleasure the narrator takes in taunting the corpse of Judge Pyncheon.[4]

William B. Dillingham has maintained that the happy ending is completely ironic.[5] Inheriting a fortune, he says, will enable Hepzibah to return to the isolated pedestal of her imaginary aristocratic rank; it will enable Clifford to retreat to his sybaritic enjoyment of appearances; while Holgrave will slide into inactivity and melancholy. This view of the ending, Dillingham says, is consonant with Hawthorne's ironic comment, in his notebook, on which he based the book: "To inherit a great fortune. To inherit a great misfortune" (Dillingham, 459).

If, however, we look at the ending of *The House of the Seven Gables* thematically and formally rather than through the lenses of biography, psychology, irony, or the supposed needs of the market, we can see enough justification for the happy conclusion. In terms of the original model, the tale of the House of Atreus in Aeschylus's *The Oresteia*, the conclusion is consonant with the working out of the curse of retribution on the divided house. The public opinion that acquits Clifford of his crime is analogous to the Athenian jury that acquits Orestes.

In spite of its Gothic overtones and historical record of darkness and tragedy, *Seven Gables* is also basically a comedy, and adheres to the conventions of comic romance. So the tale ends, as in Shakespeare's *The Tempest*, with the enemy families reconciled in the persons of Phoebe and Holgrave as with Sebastian and Miranda.

On the historical level, Hawthorne is showing that with this marriage, the democratic strain—for both Phoebe and Holgrave belong to the common people, not to the aristocratic minority—has triumphed over the decayed hierarchy that represents the dead hand of the colonial past. America has at last transcended its subservient role with respect to Europe (Judge Pyncheon's son symbolically dies there) and can emerge psychologically as well as politically as an independent power.

Parallel to this development is the theme of paradise regained. In the chapter called "The Flower of Eden" Holgrave is dismayed and disheartened by the discovery of the dead body of Judge Pyncheon; he feels this incident marks the end of his youth. Only the appearance of Phoebe saves him from despair. She, too, is quickly matured by the knowledge of this death, and confesses her love to Holgrave. "They were conscious," the narrator comments, "of nothing sad nor old. They transfigured the earth, and made it Eden again, and themselves the two first dwellers in it. The dead man, so close beside them, was forgotten. At such a crisis, there is no Death; for immortality is revealed anew, and embraces everything in its hallowed atmosphere" (307). This is unmistakably the doctrine of *felix culpa,* the fortunate fall, by which mankind, through knowledge of sin and death, through love and by Christ's redemption, regains access to paradise.

The other analogy of this action is with *The Pilgrim's Progress,* in which Christian fights through travail and doubt to the Celestial City. Even more explicitly, the plot is analogous to that of the second part of *The Pilgrim's Progress* in which Christian's wife, Christiana, also reaches the Father's house after a long and dangerous journey.

Dillingham in asserting that the ending of *The House of the Seven Gables* is ironic has to ignore these symbolic and allegorical meanings in the text. He also has to contradict Hawthorne's explicit statements that Clifford does not sink back into his former apathy and that Holgrave reaches at least a modified state of happiness.

Hawthorne was, however, far too subtle an artist not to shade this happy ending. Just as Shakespeare has his unregenerate Caliban contribute his bale to the last act of *The Tempest,* so Hawthorne leaves the old house still standing as a powerful symbol of the past. Moreover, Holgrave's transformation has its cost, as he himself recognizes: while he looks forward to planting trees, building fences and even a house for future generations to live in, he recognizes also that "'the world owes all its onward impulse to men ill at ease'" (306). There will be no more venturing journeys or radical thoughts from him. The reader is reminded of the ending of *The Blithedale Romance,* in which the formerly strong-willed reformer, Hollingsworth, is led away captive by the frail maiden, Priscilla, as with a silken noose.

The fault of the ending of *The House of the Seven Gables* is that the reader is not adequately prepared for the conversion of Holgrave— either psychologically or in terms of the plot. There are hints, it is true, of his forthcoming conversion in earlier chapters, but these are not fleshed out. He falls too quickly and complacently into the role of property holder and conservative. This is not to say that he is all set to become another grasping capitalist like the Judge. Hawthorne has shown him as a man of conscience and principle, and is likely modeling him on the kind of property-owning agrarian on which Thomas Jefferson based his ideal for the new republic of the United States as it emerged from beneath the colonial yoke of England. Although perhaps inadequately prepared for his new role, with Phoebe's help Holgrave appears ready to start becoming an ideal father figure, loving, responsible, and well positioned to become a leading figure in his New England community.

notes and references

1. Life and Letters

1. Herman Melville, "Hawthorne and His Mosses," *Literary World* 7 (17 and 25 August 1850): 120–25, 145–47; reprinted in *The Writings of Herman Melville*, vol. 9, ed. Harrison Hayford et al., Northwest-Newbury Edition (Evanston and Chicago: Northwestern University Press), 243.

2. The Importance of the Work

1. Evert Duyckinck, *Literary World* 8 (26 April 1851): 334–35; reprinted in NCE, 353.

2. Henry James, *Hawthorne*, ed. with an introduction by Tony Tanner (1879; London: Macmillan, 1967), 124.

3. Critical Reception

1. Rufus Griswold, "Nathaniel Hawthorne," reprinted in *Hawthorne: The Critical Heritage*, ed. J. Donald Crowley (New York: Barnes & Noble, 1970), 207–8.

2. Henry T. Tuckerman, "Nathaniel Hawthorne," reprinted in ibid., 213.

3. Review in *Graham's Magazine*, reprinted in ibid., 197.

4. Review in *Athenaeum*, reprinted in ibid., 201–2.

5. William Brighty Rand, "Nathaniel Hawthorne," reprinted in ibid., 482.

6. Leslie Stephen, "Nathaniel Hawthorne," reprinted in ibid., 488.

7. Anthony Trollope, review in *North American Review*, reprinted in ibid., 519.

8. Quoted in *Hawthorne among His Contemporaries*, ed. K. W. Cameron (Hartford, Conn.: Transcendental Books, 1968), 314.

9. James, *Hawthorne*, 124.

10. Quoted in by Herbert Howarth in his *Notes on Some Figures behind T. S. Eliot* (Boston: Houghton Mifflin, 1964), 221.

11. D. H. Lawrence, *Studies in Classic American Literature* (1923; New York: Viking, 1964), 83.

12. "Hawthorne and His Mosses," in *The Writings of Herman Melville,* 9:243.

13. F. O. Matthiessen, *American Renaissance: Art and Expression in the Age of Emerson and Whitman* (New York: Oxford University Press, 1941), 331.

14. Randall Stewart, *Nathaniel Hawthorne: A Biography* (New Haven, Conn.: Yale University Press, 1948), chap. 11.

15. Hyatt H. Waggoner, *Hawthorne: A Critical Study* (1955; rev. ed., Cambridge, Mass.: Harvard University Press, 1963), 187.

16. R. W. B. Lewis, *The American Adam: Innocence, Tragedy, and Tradition in the Nineteenth Century* (Chicago: University of Chicago Press, 1955), 115.

17. Leslie Fiedler, *Love and Death in the American Novel* (1960; rev. ed., New York: Stein & Day, 1966), 444.

18. Frederick C. Crews, *The Sins of the Fathers: Hawthorne's Psychological Themes* (New York: Oxford University Press, 1966), 4–6.

19. Hugo McPherson, *Hawthorne as Mythmaker* (Toronto: University of Toronto Press, 1969).

20. Nina Baym, *The Shape of Hawthorne's Career* (Ithaca, N.Y.: Cornell University Press, 1976), 8.

21. Sacvan Bercovitch, *The American Jeremiad* (Madison: University of Wisconsin Press, 1978), xii.

4. Personal Background and Sources

1. This family history is narrated by Crews in *The Sins of the Fathers,* 33–38.

2. Julian Smith, "A Hawthorne Source for *The House of the Seven Gables,*" *American Transcendental Quarterly* 1 (Spring 1969): 18–19. These *Legends of the Province House* are collected in *Works,* vol 1.

5. Literary Background: The House of Many Meanings

1. See Paul Elmer More, "The Solitude of Nathaniel Hawthorne," in *Shelburne Essays,* 1st ser. (Boston: Houghton Mifflin, 1905), 39–40; Matthiessen, *American Renaissance,* 338–40; and, most comprehensively, James

Notes and References

W. Mathews, "*The House of Atreus* and *The House of the Seven Gables*," *Emerson Society Quarterly* 63 (Spring, 1971):31–36.

2. Edmund Spenser, *The Faerie Queene*, vol. 1, ed. P. C. Bayley (Oxford: Oxford University Press, 1966), 97. See Randall Stewart's article on this topic, "Hawthorne and *The Faerie Queene*," *Philological Quarterly* 12 (1933): 196–206, and Hazel T. Emry, "Two Houses of Pride, Spenser's and Hawthorne's," *Philological Quarterly* 33 (January 1954):91–94.

3. John Bunyan, *The Pilgrim's Progress*, ed. with an introduction by Roger Sharrock (Harmondsworth: Penguin Books, 1965).

4. Helen Archibald Clarke, *Hawthorne's Country* (New York: Baker & Taylor, Co., 1910).

5. Henry James, *The American Scene* (London: Chapman & Hall, 1907), 271.

6. Gothic Romance and the Plot

1. William Bysshe Stein, *Hawthorne's Faust: A Study of the Devil Archetype* (New York: Archon Books, 1968).

7. History and Modernity

1. Matthiessen, *American Renaissance*, 322.

2. Julian Hawthorne, *Nathaniel Hawthorne and His Wife: A Biography*, vol. 1 (1884; New York: Archon Books, 1968), 391.

3. Quoted in Matthiessen, *American Renaissance*, 323.

4. Henry David Thoreau, *Walden and Civil Disobedience*, ed. Owen Thomas (New York: W.W. Norton, 1966), 82–83.

5. Leo Marx, *The Machine in the Garden: Technology and the Pastoral Ideal in America* (New York: Oxford University Press, 1964).

8. Happy Endings?

1. Julian Hawthorne, *Nathaniel Hawthorne and His Wife*, 1:383.

2. Ibid., 1:387–88.

3. *The Writings of Herman Melville*, 9:243.

9. The Bible

1. Evert Duyckinck, *Literary World* 8 (26 April 1851): 334–35; reprinted in NCE, 351.

2. Carol Schoen, "The House of the Seven Deadly Sins," *ESQ* 19 (First Quarter 1973): 26–33.

3. I owe many of these biblical references to Andrew Gutteridg's unpublished Simon Fraser University M.A. thesis, *The Scarlet Thread: Nathaniel Hawthorne's Typological and Analogical Context,* 1990.

10. The Narrative: Intention and Design

1. Yvor Winters, *In Defense of Reason* (New York: Swallow Press, 1947), 170.

2. Darrel Abel, *The Moral Picturesque: Studies in Hawthorne's Fiction* (West Lafayette, Ind.: Purdue University Press, 1988), 35.

3. Gordon Hutner, *Secrets and Sympathy: Forms of Disclosure in Hawthorne's Novels* (Athens: University of Georgia Press, 1988), 86.

11. The Characters

1. Martin Karlow, "Hawthorne's 'Modern Psychology': Madness and Its Method in *The House of the Seven Gables,*" *Bucknell Review* 27, no. 2 (1983):108–31.

2. Donald Junkins, "Hawthorne's *House of the Seven Gables:* A Prototype of the Human Mind," *Literature and Psychology* 17 (1967):209.

3. Richard Harter Fogle, "Nathaniel Hawthorne: *The House of the Seven Gables,*" in *Landmarks of American Writing,* ed. Hennig Cohen (New York: Basic Books, 1969), 111–20.

12. Structure, Style, and Emblem and Symbol

1. Abel, *The Moral Picturesque,* 255.

13. The Problem of the Conclusion

1. Alfred H. Marks, "Who Killed Judge Pyncheon? The Role of the Imagination in *The House of the Seven Gables,* reprinted in NCE, 413–28.

2. William Charvat, introduction to *The House of the Seven Gables,* in

Notes and References

The Centenary Edition of the Works of Nathaniel Hawthorne, vol. 2 (Columbus: Ohio State University Press, 1965), xxii.

3. Marcus Cunliffe, "The House of the Seven Gables," in Hawthorne Centenary Essays, ed. Roy Harvey Pearce (Columbus: Ohio State University Press, 1964), 86.

4. Crews, The Sins of the Fathers, 174–75.

5. William B. Dillingham, "Structure and Theme in The House of the Seven Gables," reprinted in NCE, 449–50.

selected bibliography

Primary Works

"The American Notebooks," by Nathaniel Hawthorne. Based upon the Original Manuscripts in the Pierpont Morgan Library. Edited by Randall Stewart. New Haven, Conn.: Yale University Press, 1932.

The Centenary Edition of the Works of Nathaniel Hawthorne. 18 vols. Edited by William Charvat et al. Columbus: Ohio State University Press, 1962–85. Includes the letters.

The Blithedale Romance: An Authoritative Text, Backgrounds and Sources, Criticism. Edited by Seymour L. Gross and Rosalie Murphy. New York: W. W. Norton, 1978.

The House of the Seven Gables: An Authoritative Text, Backgrounds and Sources, Essays in Criticism. Edited by Seymour L. Gross. New York: W. W. Norton, 1967.

The Scarlet Letter: An Authoritative Text, Essays in Criticism and Scholarship. 3d ed. Edited by Seymour L. Gross, Sculley Bradley, Richmond Croom Beatty, and E. Hudson Long. New York: W. W. Norton, 1988.

The Works of Nathaniel Hawthorne. Introductory notes by George Parsons Lathrop. 13 vols. Boston: Houghton Mifflin, 1883.

Secondary Works

Books

Abel, Darrel. The Moral Picturesque: Studies in Hawthorne's Fiction. West Lafayette, Ind.: Purdue University Press, 1988. Acute studies of structural and moral ideas in Hawthorne's long and short fiction.

Selected Bibliography

Arvin, Newton. *Hawthorne*. New York: Russell & Russell, 1961. Brief, clear, unannotated biography.

Aeschylus. *Oresteia: Agamemnon, The Libation Bearers, The Eumenides*. Translated and with an introduction by Richmond Lattimore. Chicago: University of Chicago Press, 1953. Likely sources for themes in *The House of the Seven Gables*.

Baym, Nina. *The Shape of Hawthorne's Career*. Ithaca, N.Y.: Cornell University Press, 1976. Comprehensive, structuralist approach.

Bell, Michael. *Hawthorne and the Historical Romance of New England*. Princeton, N.J.: Princeton University Press, 1971. Good study of Hawthorne's sources and his transformation of them in his work.

Bell, Millicent. *Hawthorne's View of the Artist*. Albany: State University of New York Press, 1962. Good study of Hawthorne's ambivalent view of the writer and painter.

Bercovitch, Sacvan. *The American Jeremiad*. Madison: University of Wisconsin Press, 1978. Historical survey of Jeremiad, its transformation into literature, and Hawthorne's relationship to the tradition.

Brodhead, Richard. *Hawthorne, Melville, and the Novel*. Chicago: University of Chicago Press, 1976. An analysis of the tension between the imaginative vision of these writers and the form in which they chose to work.

Bunyan, John. *The Pilgrim's Progress*. Edited with an introduction by Roger Sharrock. Harmondsworth: Penguin Books, 1965. Essential source for *The House of the Seven Gables*.

Cameron, K. W. *Hawthorne among His Contemporaries*. Hartford, Conn.: Transcendental Books, 1968. Gigantic, uneven collection of reviews, anecdotes, table talk, illustrations, and so forth, mostly in Hawthorne's time or shortly after.

Chase, Richard. *The American Novel and Its Tradition*. New York: Doubleday, 1957. Important book on the centrality of the romance in American fiction, including discussion of Hawthorne's work.

Clarke, Helen Archibald. *Hawthorne's Country*. New York: Baker & Taylor Co., 1910. Anecdotal, and sometimes trivial, material about the countries, towns, and villages where Hawthorne set his fiction.

Crews, Frederick C. *Out of My System: Psychoanalysis, Ideology, and Critical Method*. New York: Oxford University Press, 1975. Good defense of psychoanalytic criticism.

———. *The Sins of the Fathers: Hawthorne's Psychological Themes*. New York: Oxford University Press, 1966. Illuminating and essential Freudian reading of Hawthorne's work.

Crowley, J. Donald, ed. *Hawthorne: The Critical Heritage*. New York: Barnes & Noble, 1970. Anthology of critical essays and reviews up to 1879.

Davidson, Edward H. *Hawthorne's Last Phase*. New Haven, Conn.: Yale

University Press, 1949. Analysis of Hawthorne's decline as a writer in his later years.

Doubleday, Neal Frank. *Hawthorne's Early Tales: A Critical Study.* New Haven, Conn.: Yale University Press, 1972. Good study of early work before the novels.

Elder, Marjorie. *Nathaniel Hawthorne: Transcendental Symbolist.* Athens: Ohio University Press, 1969. Discussion of Hawthorne's connections with American transcendentalists and their symbolic method.

Feidelson, Charles, Jr. *Symbolism and American Literature.* Chicago: University of Chicago Press, 1953. Early but still valuable study of symbolic movement in American literature.

Fiedler, Leslie. *Love and Death in the American Novel.* 1960; rev. ed., New York: Stein & Day, 1966. Lawrentian and contentious study of the subversive and submissive elements in American literature.

Fogle, Richard Harter. *Hawthorne's Fiction: The Light and the Dark.* Norman: University of Oklahoma Press, 1952. Good early study of Hawthorne's symbolic use of chiaroscuro.

Gollin, Rita. *Nathaniel Hawthorne and the Truth of Dreams.* Baton Rouge: Louisiana State University Press, 1979. The role of dreams and literary dream forms in his work.

Hawthorne, Julian. *Nathaniel Hawthorne and His Wife: A Biography.* 1884; reprint, New York: Archon Books, 1968. Uncritical, anecdotal, double biographical portrait, largely through letters.

Hutner, Gordon. *Secrets and Sympathy: Forms of Disclosure in Hawthorne's Novels.* Athens: University of Georgia Press, 1988. Discusses Hawthorne's use of Gothic devices, such as the secret, for complex fictional purposes.

James, Henry. *The American Scene.* London: Chapman & Hall, 1907. Contains a nostalgic and beautifully written sketch of Hawthorne's Salem.

———. *Hawthorne.* New York: Harper's, 1879; reprinted (edited with an introduction by Tony Tanner), London: Macmillan, 1967. Classic early short study, more biographical than critical.

Lawrence, D. H. *Studies in Classic American Literature.* New York: Thomas Seltzer, 1923; reprinted, Viking, 1964. Revolutionary rereading of the American literary tradition, concentrating on the demonic and disintegrative elements in the work of Hawthorne and other classic American writers.

Lewis, R. W. B. *The American Adam: Innocence, Tragedy, and Tradition in the Nineteenth Century.* Chicago: University of Chicago Press, 1955. Important contribution to myth criticism.

Lundblad, Jane. *Nathaniel Hawthorne and the Tradition of Gothic Romance.* New York: Haskell House, 1964. Pedestrian survey of Hawthorne's debts to Gothic Romance in Europe and America.

Selected Bibliography

McPherson, Hugo. *Hawthorne as Mythmaker.* Toronto: University of Toronto Press, 1969. Valuable study of Hawthorne's personality and personal myth.

Male, Roy R. *Hawthorne's Tragic Vision.* Austin: University of Texas Press, 1957. Study of Hawthorne's tragic vision in relation to the Christian tradition.

Marx, Leo. *The Machine in the Garden: Technology and the Pastoral Ideal in America.* New York: Oxford University Press, 1964. Seminal study of the role of the machine in changing the moral and literary landscape from 1840 on.

Matthiessen, F. O. *American Renaissance.* New York: Oxford University Press, 1941. Seminal early study of Hawthorne's roots and relationship to Emerson, Thoreau, and Melville.

Scholes, Robert. *Structuralism in Literature: An Introduction.* New Haven, Conn.: Yale University Press, 1974. Clear introduction to this important modern critical movement.

Spenser, Edmund. *The Faerie Queene.* 2 vols. Edited by P. C. Bayley. Oxford: Oxford University Press, 1968. Strong influence on the allegorical nature of *The House of the Seven Gables.*

Stein, William Bysshe. *Hawthorne's Faust: A Study of the Devil Archetype.* New York: Archon Books, 1968. A good study of Gothic influences and the consequent significance of the Faust theme.

Stewart, Randall. *Nathaniel Hawthorne: A Biography.* New Haven, Conn.: Yale University Press, 1948. Standard biographical study, written on the principle that Hawthorne was an orthodox Christian.

Thoreau, Henry David. *Walden and Civil Disobedience.* Edited by Owen Thomas. New York: W. W. Norton, 1966. The two most famous works by the transcendentalist friend of Hawthorne, whose attitudes toward contemporary events may be profitably compared to those of the novelist.

Turner, Arlin. *Nathaniel Hawthorne: A Biography.* New York: Oxford University Press, 1980. Incorporates materials not available to Stewart and new insights.

Von Abele, Rudolph. *The Death of the Artist: A Study of Hawthorne's Disintegration.* The Hague: Martinus Nijhoff, 1957. Concentrates mainly on work after *The Marble Faun,* but is also valuable on earlier work.

Wagenknecht, Edward. *Nathaniel Hawthorne: Man and Writer.* New York: Oxford University Press, 1961. Orthodox biographical and critical study.

Waggoner, Hyatt H. *Hawthorne: A Critical Study.* Cambridge, Mass.: Harvard University Press, 1955. Attempts to pin down the religious convictions of Hawthorne behind the mask of ambiguities.

Winters, Yvor. *In Defense of Reason.* New York: Swallow Press and William Morrow, 1947. Early formulation of function of realism and romance in Hawthorne.

Articles

Arae, Jonathan. "The House and the Railroad: *Dombey and Son* and *The House of the Seven Gables.*" *New England Quarterly* 55 (March 1978):3–22.

Battaglia, Francis J. "*The House of the Seven Gables:* New Light on Old Problems." *PMLA* 82 (December 1967): 179–90.

Beebe, Maurice. "The Fall of the House of Pyncheon." *Nineteenth-Century Fiction* 11 (June 1956):1–17.

Borges, Jorge Luis. "Nathaniel Hawthorne." In *Other Inquisitions, 1937–1952*, translated by Ruth L. C. Simms. Austin: University of Texas Press, 1964.

Brownell, W. C. "Hawthorne." In *American Prose Masters*. New York: Scribner, 1909. Sensible early survey.

Buitenhuis, Peter. "Henry James on Hawthorne." *New England Quarterly* 32 (June 1959):207–25.

Caldwell, Wayne T. "The Emblem Tradition and the Symbolic Mode: Clothing Imagery in *The House of the Seven Gables.*" *ESQ* [formerly known as the *Emerson Society Quarterly*] 19 (First Quarter 1973):34–42.

Carlson, Constance H. "Wit and Irony in Hawthorne's *The House of the Seven Gables.*" In *A Handful of Spice: Essays in Maine Literature and History*, edited by Richard S. Sprague, 159–68. University of Maine Studies 88. Orono: University of Maine, 1967.

Cunliffe, Marcus. "The House of the Seven Gables." In *Hawthorne Centenary Essays*, edited by Roy Harvey Pearce, 79–101. Columbus: Ohio State University Press, 1964.

Dillingham, William B. "Structure and Theme in *The House of the Seven Gables.*" *Nineteenth-Century Fiction* 14 (June 1959):59–70.

Dooley, Patrick K. "Genteel Poverty: Hepzibah in *The House of the Seven Gables.*" *Markham Review* 9 (Fall 1979):33–35.

Dryden, Edgar. "Hawthorne's Castle in the Air: Form and Theme in *The House of the Seven Gables.*" *Journal of English Literary History* 38 (June 1971):294–317.

Emry, Hazel T. "Two Houses of Pride: Spenser's and Hawthorne's." *Philological Quarterly* 33 (January 1954):91–94.

Fogle, Richard Harter. "Nathaniel Hawthorne: *The House of the Seven Gables.*" In *Landmarks of American Writing*, ed. Hennig Cohen. New York: Basic Books, 1969.

Gatta, John. "Progress and Providence in *The House of the Seven Gables.*" *American Literature* 50 (March 1978):37–48.

Gerber, John C. "A Critical Exercise in Teaching *The House of the Seven Gables.*" *Emerson Society Quarterly* 4 (Fourth Quarter 1961):8–11.

Selected Bibliography

Gilmore, Michael T. "The Artist and the Marketplace in *The House of the Seven Gables.*" *ELH* [formerly *Journal of English Literary History*] 48 (Spring 1981):172–89.

Gray, Richard. "Hawthorne: A Problem: *The House of the Seven Gables.*" In *Nathaniel Hawthorne: New Critical Essays*, edited by Robert A. Lee, 88–109. London: Vision, 1982.

Griffith, Clark. "Substance and Shadow: Language and Meaning in *The House of the Seven Gables.*" *Modern Philology* 51 (February 1954): 187–95.

Harris, Kenneth Marc. "Judge Pyncheon's Brotherhood: Puritan Theories of Hypocrisy and *The House of the Seven Gables.*" *Nineteenth-Century Fiction* 39 (September 1984):144–62.

Hirolgo, Washizu. "Rebuilding a House: An Approach to *The House of the Seven Gables.*" *Studies in English Literature* [Tokyo] 60 (December 1983):293–309.

Horne, Lewis B. "Of Place and Time: A Note on *The House of the Seven Gables.*" *SNNTS: Studies in the Novel* [North Texas State University] 2 (1970):459–67.

Jacobs, Edward Craney. "Shakespearean Borrowings in *The House of the Seven Gables.*" *Nathaniel Hawthorne Journal* (1977):343–46.

Junkins, Donald. "Hawthorne's *The House of the Seven Gables:* A Prototype of the Human Mind." *Literature and Psychology* 17 (1967):193–210.

Karlow, Martin. "Hawthorne's 'Modern Psychology': Madness and Method in *The House of the Seven Gables.*" *Bucknell Review* 27 (1983):108–31.

Kehler, Joel R. "*The House of the Seven Gables:* House, Home, and Hawthorne's Psychology of Habitation." *ESQ* 21 (Third Quarter 1975): 142–53.

Kleiman, E. "The Wizardry of Nathaniel Hawthorne: *Seven Gables* as Fairy Tale and Parable." *English Studies in Canada* 4(Fall 1978):289–304.

Klinkowitz, Jerome. "Ending the *Seven Gables:* Old Light on a New Problem." *SNNTS: Studies in the Novel* [North Texas State University] 4 (1972):396–401.

Levy, Alfred J. "*The House of the Seven Gables:* The Religion of Love." *Nineteenth-Century Fiction* 16 (December 1961):189–203.

Levy, Leo B. "Picturesque Style in *The House of the Seven Gables.*" *New England Quarterly* 39 (June 1966):147–60.

Marks, Alfred H. "Hawthorne's Daguerreotypist: Scientist, Artist, Reformer." In *The House of the Seven Gables*, edited by Seymour L. Gross, 330–50. Norton Critical Edition. New York: W. W. Norton, 1967.

———. "Who Killed Judge Pyncheon? The Role of the Imagination in *The House of the Seven Gables.*" In *The House of the Seven Gables*, edited by Seymour L. Gross, 413–28. Norton Critical Edition, 1967.

Mathews, James W. "The House of Artreus and *The House of the Seven Gables*." *Emerson Society Quarterly* 63 (Spring 1971):31–36.

Melville, Herman. "Hawthorne and His Mosses." *Literary World* Seven (17 and 24 August 1850):125–27, 145–47. Reprinted in *The Writings of Herman Melville*, vol. 9, edited by Harrison Hayford et al. Norwest-Newbury Edition. Evanston and Chicago: Northwestern University Press, 1987.

Michelson, Bruce. "Hawthorne's House of Three Stories." *New England Quarterly* 57 (June 1984): 163–83.

More, Paul Elmer. "Hawthorne: Looking Before and After." In *Shelburne Essays*, 2d ser., 173–87. Boston: Houghton Mifflin, 1905.

Pattison, Joseph C. "'The Celestial Railroad' as Dream-Tale." *American Quarterly* 20 (Summer 1968):224–36.

———. "Point of View in Hawthorne." *PMLA* 82 (October 1967):363–69.

Pearson, Norman Holmes. "The Pynchons and Judge Pyncheon." *Essex Institute Historical Collections* 100 (October 1964):235–55.

Ringe, Donald. "Hawthorne's Psychology of the Head and Heart." *PMLA* 65 (March 1950):120–32.

Schoen, Carol. "The House of the Seven Deadly Sins." *ESQ* 19 (First Quarter 1973):26–33.

Smith, Julian. "A Hawthorne Source for *The House of the Seven Gables*." *American Transcendental Quarterly* 1 (Spring 1969):18–19.

Sterne, Richard Clark. "Hawthorne's Politics in *The House of the Seven Gables*." *Canadian Review of American Studies* 6 (Spring 1975):74–83.

Stewart, Randall. "Hawthorne and *The Faerie Queene*." *Philological Quarterly* 12 (April 1933):196–206.

———. "Melville and Hawthorne." *South Atlantic Quarterly* 51 (July 1952):436–46.

Swanson, Donald R. "On Building *The House of the Seven Gables*." *Ball State University Forum* 10 (Winter 1969):43–50.

Thomas, Brook. "*The House of the Seven Gables:* Reading the Romance of America." *PMLA* 97 (March 1982):195–211.

Warren, Austin. "Hawthorne's Reading." *New England Quarterly* 8 (December 1935):480–97.

Whelan, Robert Emmett, Jr. "*The House of the Seven Gables:* Allegory of the Heart." *Renascence* 31 (Winter 1979):67–82.

Bibliography and Reference

Jones, Buford. *A Check List of Hawthorne Criticism, 1951–1966*. Hartford, Conn.: Transcendental Books, 1967. Fairly complete listing of books and articles about Hawthorne in this period.

Ricks, Beatrice, Joseph D. Adams, and Jack O. Hazelrigg. *Nathaniel Hawthorne: A Reference Bibliography, 1900–1971*. Boston: G. K. Hall, 1972. With selected nineteenth-century materials. Most comprehensive bibliographical source for the period.

Woodress, James, ed. *Eight American Authors*. Rev. ed. New York: W. W. Norton, 1971. One of the eight is Nathaniel Hawthorne. Walter Blair compiles an annotated critical list of most of the significant commentary up to that date.

index

Index

the author

Peter Buitenhuis received his B.A. and M.A. in English language and literature from Oxford University, and his Ph.D. in American studies from Yale. He has taught at the University of Oklahoma, Yale, Wesleyan University in Connecticut, Macalester College in Minnesota, the University of Toronto, the University of California at Berkeley, McGill, and Simon Fraser University in British Columbia, where he served as chair of the department of English between 1975 and 1981.

His publications include *Five American Moderns* (1968), *Hugh MacLennan* (1968, rev. 1983), *The Grasping Imagination: The American Writings of Henry James* (1970), *E. J. Pratt and His Works* (1987), and *The Great War of Words: British, American, and Canadian Propaganda and Fiction, 1914–1933* (1987). He has edited *The Selected Poems of E. J. Pratt* (1968) and, with Ira Nadel, *George Orwell: A Reassessment* (1988). He has also written many articles and reviews on American and Canadian literature and has served as the president of the Canadian Association for American Studies and as chair of the Canadian Association of Chairmen of English.